Make Love,

Not Scrapbooks

and 9 other
research-based
love tips to intensify
your relationship

Jennifer Gill Rosier, Ph.D.

Front and back cover design by Jennifer Gill Rosier, Ph.D.
Book design by Jennifer Gill Rosier, Ph.D.
Book edited by Martha Isom Russell, M.A.

Like my book? Check out my blog…
www.JensLoveLessons.com

And, take a look at the website for this book…
www.MakeLoveNotScrapbooks.com

Printed in the United States of America
First Printing: August 2011

Published by www.Lulu.com

ISBN: 978-0-557-45802-8

for wesley

you're all i need to get by

"Love is like a plant.
You need to nurture it.
You need to continuously
work to maintain it
and make it better.
You can't just put
it in the cupboard."

~John Lennon

table of contents

Acknowledgements		ix
Introduction		xi
Chapter One	Be Supportive	1
Chapter Two	Generate Some Blushing	15
Chapter Three	Talk	23
Chapter Four	Contemplate, Decide, Astonish	39
Chapter Five	Don't Worry, Be Happy	47
Chapter Six	Laugh	59
Chapter Seven	Make Love, Not Scrapbooks	69
Chapter Eight	Heart the Hell Out of Your Mate	83
Chapter Nine	Add in a Dash of Spice	89
Chapter Ten	Manage That Conflict	97
Extra Love Tips		119
Conclusion		125
Resources for Couples		129
References		137
About the Author		149

ACKNOWLEDGEMENTS

I'd like to start by saying that I could never have started or finished this book without my remarkable husband. Understanding, supportive, and encouraging, this man has backed me in every decision that I have made over the last eleven years and has always given me the confidence to continue when I felt it was impossible. His compliments have boosted my self-esteem, assurances have made me feel secure, and affection has enabled me to believe in true love. He's my partner-in-crime, soul mate, and best friend. Thank you for being you.

Martha Isom Russell is another person to whom I am indebted. Above all else, I want to thank Marti for being one of my dearest friends. She literally is the most thoughtful, kind-hearted person I have ever met. On top of volunteering to edit this book (which was ridiculously amazing, by the way), all of the creative ideas, unconditional support, and delightfully considerate messages that she has thrown my way since we met have caused me to love her to pieces. Thank you for being incredibly glorious.

I'd also like to thank all of the people who have contributed to this book in one way or another. Specifically, I'd like to thank Amanda, April,

Brandy, Brenda, Chrissy, Debby, Elizabeth, Elyse, Erin, Heather, Jessica, Kindra, Lisa, Molly, Rebecca, Robin, Samantha, Stephanie, and Susan for all of their eloquent, honest words about their own successful relationships and marriages. Your comments have motivated me and reinforced my desire to study love for the rest of my life.

Another group of people who are near and dear to my heart are the educators who seriously impacted my life in extremely positive ways throughout my 11-year stint in higher education. In particular, Dr. Laura Janusik inspired me, Dr. Brant Burleson believed in me, Dr. Andy Wolvin stood up for me, Dr. Jim Tyler made me think, Dr. Margaret Fitch-Hauser helped me organize my ideas, Dr. Susan Brinson opened my eyes, and they all caused me to question the world in a new and interesting way. Thank you.

Last, but certainly not least, I want to thank my Mom and Dad for showing me what a good marriage looks like. It certainly wasn't perfect, but it was a damn good prototype. I may not have been able to find love myself if I didn't have great love right at home to model. I would not be who I am or where I am today without the two of you. And for that, I am eternally grateful.

×

introduction

W hen I first tell people that I wrote a book (you know, the one you're reading right now), they always ask me about the origin of the title. "Where did you come up with *that?*" they say. Luckily, I always have an answer.

First of all, for the majority of my life, I've held the belief that relationships (successful relationships) are hard work. They require a significant amount of time and effort from both people involved. From honing your ability to engage in effective conflict about who's turn it is to do the dishes, to figuring out how to balance your work life with your home life, to crafting messages that skillfully reveal your deepest darkest secrets without embarrassing anyone, trying to make your relationship succeed can be exceedingly exhausting and overwhelming. And those of you who put in the necessary man-hours initiating, intensifying, managing, and repairing your relationship tend to experience greater satisfaction in the end.

When you start a relationship with another person, it's important to realize that your lifestyle is going to change. You can't expect to still hang out with your friends as often, spend as much money, or have as many hobbies (among other things) as you did before you had a plus one. The energy that you once put towards your daily routine needs to be divvied up differently. You have to figure out how to cut the cake that is your life so that your partner gets a nice fat slice. The bottom line: you need to be willing to seriously dedicate yourself to your relationship. And, you're going to have to sacrifice a few things to do so.

Second, before I started writing this book, Hus (my husband) and I were tossing around title ideas.* We came up with all kinds of crazy things. And then, "Make Love, Not War" was thrown into the mix. I liked it. But clearly, my book had nothing to do with war. I started to think about how I could alter the popular phrase to my advantage. So, I thought about activities that people engage in that take time away from the more important things in life—their relationships with other human beings. I Googled, "most popular female (because I figured that women would be more likely to read my book) hobbies."

Quilting, blogging, baking, and running were common results. I felt like I was onto something, but "make love, not quilts" just didn't sound right. I scrolled down and saw it—one of *my own* favorite pastimes: scrapbooking. I gave it a whirl: *Make Love, Not Scrapbooks*. It had a nice ring to it. I continued reading about this common interest among women.

Apparently, gluing photos to paper with ribbons, stickers, and glitter is a HUGE deal, with the scrapbooking industry doubling in size between 2001 and 2004 to $2.5 billion! In fact, the Craft and Hobby Association named scrapbooking as America's most popular hobby. And, it's estimated that there is at least one scrapbooker in 32.5 million American households. It's actually quite impressive.

So, I'm sorry if you picked up this book because you were expecting to learn about how to creatively coordinate paper patterns, use various embellishments to enhance your photos, or make your own stickers with your recently purchased Cricut. You won't find any of that here. But don't fret. I think you should still read it; it's still pretty useful.

Okay, so back to the origin of the title. I let my newly created title marinate in my mind for a few months. Once I decided that this was it, I started to realize the multiple meanings behind the title. Clearly, the aim of the book is to get my readers thinking about spending more time with their partners and less time doing all of those trivial things in life that we love so much; like scrapbooking. Not only do I want to encourage you to

---

* Side note: for some reason, I always have to figure out the title of whatever I'm working on (i.e. a book, paper, journal article, blog post, etc.) before I begin writing. I have no idea why I do this; it's just the way it is.

put more effort into your relationship, but I also want you to do it (you know: get it on, ride the flag pole, do the nasty, stuff the turkey)† on a much more regular basis. The fact of the matter (as you'll read more about in chapter seven) is that many romantically involved Americans have terribly dissatisfying sex lives. Thus, *Make Love, Not Scrapbooks* is not just the title of the book, but it's also one of the ten love tips described in the next 150 pages.

Whether you feel like your relationship is perfectly fine, needs a little assistance, or is on its last leg, this book can help you. Think of it like an instruction manual for your relationship; you can always use it to trouble-shoot problems, but even when everything seems to be working out, you can still use it to scan for some routine maintenance strategies. In the end, my hope is that you can turn to this book whenever your relationship needs a little pick-me-up, you want some romantic ideas about what to do this weekend, or you need help repairing some serious damage.

Like I said, relationships are hard work; they don't just maintain themselves. So, even if you feel like your relationship is good-to-go, learning about and implementing some of these behaviors into your daily life can definitely intensify your seemingly perfect romance. And unfortunately, it won't always be perfect.

While each chapter can clearly stand alone as an individual piece of advice about a certain relationship-boosting technique, behavior, or activity, you'll find the greatest positive impact on your relationship when you collectively utilize all of the advice found in this book.

As a graduate student at Purdue University, I set out to write a book that would combine real relationship research and real life experiences in an interesting and significant way. I wanted my readers to have a clear set of substantial, easy-to-understand, relatable love tips that they could use to make their lives better. Based on an extensive literature review of the subject, knowledge gained from my three higher education degrees, my own personal experience with the love of my life (Hus), and many conversations with a group of wonderfully eloquent individuals involved in their own successful relationships, I wrote. And wrote. And wrote.

A few years, a doctoral degree, and two children (twins!) later, I completed what you have in your hands today. And now I would like to present to you my labor of love; a book that encourages you to *Make Love, Not Scrapbooks*.

---

† C'mon people, I want you to have more sex.

chapter one: Be supportive

"I'm on your team." A few years ago, I heard one of my best friends say this very sentence to her husband. They were talking about something... yadda yadda yadda... and he felt like she wasn't on his side. She said to him, "Honey, I'm on your team." He smiled and replied, "I know." Since that day, I've heard her say this many more times. It expresses her commitment to their bond, and it lets her husband know that in the end, she's always got his back. If you take a minute to think about it, it's actually a really important sentence to say every now and then. In fact, I think that this sentence is so important that it has become one of my relationship mantras over the last few years.

When I emailed my best friend about how much her conversation impacted me, she wrote back, "That was a turning point in my marriage where I was awakened and finally understood the importance of being on the same team. I realized that although I sometimes may have strong opinions about something, it is more important to be supportive than to always be right." Her insight about the inner workings of marriage continues to influence how I view relationships to this day.

At a certain point in any relationship, people begin to integrate their separate lives into a shared life. You start combining your lives physically, emotionally, and communicatively. You may use "we" language, plan your days and nights around each other's schedules, develop joint attitudes and beliefs, and maybe even move in together or get married. Once you enter this stage, there's usually some sort of understood commitment between the two of you. This is where being on the same team and showing unconditional support for one another becomes more evident as an important tool to maintain your relationship.

Social support researchers[1] have explained that support can be *instrumental* (by offering goods or services to your partner) or *emotional* (by offering your partner love or understanding). And, in their 2001 study published in the *Western Journal of Nursing Research*, M. Cynthia Logsdon, DNS, ARNP and Dr. Wayne Usui, Ph.D., theorized that the type of support that you dish out is most beneficial if it matches your partner's needs.[2] For example, let's say that your husband is suffering after the loss of a good friend and he needs you to be empathetic and compassionate. Some of you may decide to fulfill that need by listening to him talk about his friend's life, their friendship, and anything else he wants to discuss about this difficult time. You might also tell him that you probably would feel the same way if you were in that situation, and that it's perfectly natural for him to have these feelings. On the other hand, some of you might decide to strategically avoid the discussion all together (maybe because you think it's awkward, you think that your husband doesn't want to talk about it, or you're scared to talk about death yourself). In hopes that you can make your partner feel better, you decide to make arrangements (i.e. you order the plane tickets, take off work so that you can stay home with the kids, you know, the usual stuff) so that he can go to the funeral. Both of these options would show your support for him. But, since he actually needed some *emotional* support instead of *instrumental* support, the former is more likely to help him feel better.

> "My husband is the most supportive person I have ever met. He just wants me to be happy and he really means that. Whatever I want to do, whoever I want to be, he's behind me 100%. I don't even have to ask; I just know."
>
> *–Erin, in a relationship with Andy since January 2003 & married since May 2007*

Once you've figured out what your mate needs from you (i.e. *instrumental* or *emotional* support), you can start dishing out the good stuff.

But, providing **good** support is sometimes difficult to do. In fact, it's really difficult. Not because we don't want to support our partners, but because most of us don't know *how* to provide effective support; we don't know what it looks like. Support can involve physically being there for your girlfriend when she needs you, listening to your husband's concerns about life, providing encouragement to your wife, building up your partner's self-esteem, comforting your boyfriend when he's upset, or actually giving your mate direct assistance and help when it's wanted. To further complicate things, your supportive responses will likely look very different based on the situation and topic of conversation. And, it's not enough to just say, "I support you." I mean, it helps, but you want to also *show* your partner that when it comes down to it, you will be there through thick and thin and that you'll be on your mate's side when push comes to shove. It's really quite complex. Overall, you want to support your partner during times of distress, times of decision, and all of those times in between.

IN TIMES OF DISTRESS

Imagine this familiar scenario: it's Friday night and you have a big *Guy's Night Out* planned (Side Note: If you are a woman reading this book, don't worry, a familiar example for you is on its way). You and your friends are pre-gaming (drinking before you go out) at your place when your wife walks in the door in tears. She says that she has just lost her job. What do you do? Do you cancel *Guy's Night Out* to stay home and talk it out or do you quickly tell your mate that she'll be okay and leave her a bottle of wine? How do you support your wife during her time of distress?

Okay ladies, here's your scenario. Unlike the above example, your familiar support interaction involves you and your best friend (not because men don't need or want support but because I think that this example is much more common and will help you better understand how to create an effective response--for anyone in your life). Imagine this: it's Friday night and you have big plans. You're getting ready at home, when your best friend calls to say that she just broke up with her boyfriend and she's on her way over. When your best friend arrives at your house, you can tell that she has been crying a lot. You say, "Tell me what happened." Your friend begins to sob while she tells you all about the breakup. She says that last week she found out that her boyfriend of 2 years had been having an affair for the last SIX months and that she broke up with him during an argument that night. How do you comfort your devastated friend?

Before I went to graduate school, my response to either of these scenarios would have been something like, "I can't believe this happened to you! Your boss/boyfriend is such a freaking jerk! I know it sucks now, but you're *so* much better without that job/him. You can get through this. That job/He is *not* worth your tears."

After reading some social support research, however, I quickly learned that this is a **horrible** way to comfort someone. Unfortunately, I gave support like this to many people before I learned how to *actually* be supportive.

As explained in a considerably large body of research, one of the best ways to be supportive during distressful times is to make your messages *person-centered*. Person-centeredness refers to the extent to which messages "explicitly acknowledge, elaborate, legitimize, and contextualize the feelings and perspective of a distressed other."[3] Individuals who are providing support to another person should try to make their messages high in person-centeredness. Below are some steps to creating person-centered emotional support developed by Dr. Brant Burleson, Ph.D., a leading scholar in the field of emotional support research.[4]

7 Steps to Providing Emotional Support

Motivate the distressed person to tell and retell his or her story. Here, you can say things like, "Tell me what happened," and "I want to know everything." Let them know that you are there to listen to **whatever** they want to tell you. Then, you need to actually sit there for as long as your partner needs you.

Encourage the expression of thoughts and feelings. Here, you want to get them to talk about how the distressful event made them feel. They should talk about the thoughts and feelings that they experienced during and after the situation being described. This will help them work things out in their head. You could say things like, "How did you feel when he said that?" "Were there any signs?" or "What do you think might have led up to this?"

Legitimize the distressed person's thoughts and feelings. Tell and show your partner that it's completely normal and expected for them to feel the way that they do. Say things like, "It's okay to cry," "It's totally normal to feel this way," "I think these are really typical feelings to have," and "It's perfectly fine to be angry, sad, etc."

Ask questions about the problem. You want to ask questions so your distressed partner can elaborate and so that you can fully understand what happened. You could ask, "What happened after you confronted him?" or "Did she say why she fired you?" Plus, when you ask clarifying questions during a conversation, it really makes people feel like you care about what they're saying.

Be actively engaged in the conversation. You want to be sure to use vocal verifiers like "uh-huh" and "yeah" to show that you're listening. Also, maintain eye contact, smile (or frown), and nod your head to show understanding. Basically, you need to be present in the moment.

Reinforce your mate's feelings and emotions. You want your partner to know that they aren't crazy for feeling this way. Connect your mate's feelings to the distressful event. "Something like this would definitely make anyone feel this way," and "I totally understand why you would feel that way."

Let your partner know that you understand. Empathize with your partner. You could say, "I would feel the same way *if* this happened to me." But be careful that you don't insert your own experience here. Keep it at just understanding how you *would* feel if this happened to you and stay away from, "I felt this way last year when I lost my job." You only want to give examples from your own life *if your partner asks you.*

If you can follow these steps, you'll be on your way to providing effective support while hopefully alleviating some of your mate's distress in the process. It's important to note that the goal of these interactions is not to make your partner feel *completely* better; some distressful events require a good amount of support and *time* to overcome. You may not be able to accomplish this goal in one interaction. But, you do have the ability to help your partner work out some of their thoughts and feelings about the event, which could then allow the person you love to feel a little, and sometimes *a lot*, better.

Like many things in life, the best way to become an expert comforter is to analyze your personal experiences and practice creating your own messages. Think about all of those past interactions when you were comforted by someone else. Who was comforting you? What did this person say or do that made you feel better? What did he or she say or do that made you feel worse? Evaluate a few comforting interactions from your past. You'll probably find some common characteristics of good and bad supportive interactions. Next, review the seven steps previously mentioned and the list of supportive interaction characteristics you just created. Start thinking about how you would respond to real situations you might have with your partner. How would you comfort your mate after a job loss, a fight with a good friend, or the death of a parent? You can never anticipate all of the circumstances associated with supporting your mate during a distressing time, but you *can* try to create some key sentences that you would like to say during most, if not all, conversations where your significant other is suffering emotionally. In his chapter entitled "Comforting as everyday social support" in Dr. Steve Duck, Ph.D., and Dr. Roxane Silver's, Ph.D., 1990 book about support in personal relationships, Dr. Brant Burleson, Ph.D., identified comforting our partners (and anyone!) in times of distress as a key relationship maintenance behavior.[5] And many other researchers[6] have claimed that effective comforting has the potential to significantly enhance you and your partner's feelings of satisfaction, closeness, trust, and intimacy. In addition, some studies have even revealed that people tend to report emotional support as the most desired type of support provided by relationship partners.[7]

To help you further develop successful comforting conversations, here are 5 things that you should AVOID when providing support.

5 Things to Avoid

DO NOT discuss your own experiences. This takes the focus away from your mate and puts it on you, which you don't want to do. This conversation is all about your partner; what happened to them and their feelings about what happened. It's not about you. Avoid saying things like, "I understand. I felt this way when this happened to me a few months ago." The only time that it would be acceptable to insert your own experience is if your mate asks you to do so. But even then, you should refrain from taking over too much of the conversation; less than one minute of talk-time dedicated to your experience should suffice.

DO NOT ignore your partner's feelings. Trying to help your mate look at the bright side may seem like a good idea, but it doesn't always help them feel better. Saying, "Well, at least you have great friends!" or "Don't worry, another job will come around!" makes the distressed person feel like their thoughts about the situation do not matter and that they should not feel sad, angry, or upset because it's not that big of a deal. News flash: IT'S A BIG DEAL. If your partner is upset about it, it's a big deal. Treat the situation as if it is serious; even if you don't think it is.

DO NOT tell your partner what they should do or how they should feel. This seems pretty obvious, but many people (including myself) sometimes feel the urge to tell their friend or partner what to do. Does this sound familiar? "Quit crying. He's not worth *your* tears" or "All you need to do is get out there tomorrow morning to look for your next perfect job!" Unless the distressed person asks for advice, you should *never* offer any. Keep your thoughts about what they should or should not do to yourself. And, if your partner *does* ask, make sure that you remain positive, non evaluative, and brief. Try to help your partner problem solve the situation on his/her own. You can give a little input, but remember, this is about the other person; it's not about you.

DO NOT evaluate. Whatever you do, make sure that you don't evaluate the other people involved in the situation. Ever. When you say to your crying best friend, "You're *so* much better than him. He was a jerk anyway," you're basically stating that she wasted her time with her boyfriend who she likely had very strong feelings for. It makes her feel foolish for being with him and for loving him, which could lower her self-esteem. This can easily be applied to any other situation as well. Telling your wife, "That job wasn't a good fit for you; you were above that job," makes her feel stupid for even taking that job in the first place. Why did she stay there for as long as she did if it wasn't a good job for her? Remember that your best friend is sad because she loved her boyfriend and that your wife is upset because she probably liked her job. Don't demean your partner's decisions by evaluating the situation or the other people involved.

DO NOT distract their attention away from your partner's feelings. You know this one: "Let's forget about this and go out for a beer." While some people may like to forget about the situation momentarily and go out drinking, doing so will ultimately not alleviate any of their sadness or anger about what happened to them. When we're hit with a difficult experience that brings us anguish, we need to work things out (figure out why it happened, how we feel about it, what we are going to do next) in order to *truly* feel better. And, talking about the situation and our feelings about the situation will help us get back to that happy place a lot sooner. Let your partner talk it out for as long as they want.

This is not the *only* way to comfort your spouse. You two may have some additional relationship-specific ways to comfort one another. For instance, maybe your wife really likes to veg-out and watch a movie with you after talking about her problems. Or, maybe your boyfriend likes to briefly talk about his problem at first and then revisit it later when he feels like he's calmed down a bit. Whatever it is, use your knowledge about your partner's emotional support preferences when following the guidelines previously discussed. Anytime that your partner is feeling sad, lonely, angry, or depressed, make sure that you follow the rules described here by actively listening, encouraging elaboration, validating feelings, and whatever you do, don't call your best friend's boyfriend or your wife's boss a freaking jerk!

IN TIMES OF DECISION

In the first few years of my relationship with Hus (my husband), I was working towards my Bachelor's degree at the University of Maryland, College Park. Our families lived nearby (Hus and I are originally from Montgomery County, MD and Prince George's County, MD, respectively) and we were able to see our friends whenever we wanted (since they also lived nearby). About four years into our relationship, I told Hus that I wanted to go to graduate school. I explained that if I went, I (and hopefully Hus) would need to move wherever I was accepted, away from all of our family and friends. At first, he was in shock. But after a little bit of time, Hus said, "I know this is important to you, and I will come with you wherever you want to go." I was relieved.

> "My husband makes me feel like I can accomplish anything I put my mind to and encourages me to pursue my dreams. I like to think that I reciprocate this. His support makes me feel important, empowered, and in the end I accomplish so much more than I might have without it."
>
> –Rachel, in a relationship with Jacob since October 2001 & married since January 2010

That summer, we moved 13 hours away to Auburn, Alabama. This was a big step in our relationship. Not only did Hus decide to let me follow my dreams by uprooting his own life, but we moved so far away that we were only able to visit Maryland 3-4 times a year. We didn't have the luxury of spontaneously hanging out with our friends and we couldn't just have our family members over for dinner on a Tuesday night anymore. This was an adjustment (and let's be serious, moving from a large Mid-Atlantic city to a small Southern town was an adjustment, too). But Hus was unconditionally supportive of my desire to relocate for my education. His continued endorsement of this big change in our life made me feel truly loved, understood, and secure.

A short couple of years later, it was time to apply for Ph.D. programs. I knew this was going to be a hard sell. Hus and I had initially decided to move back to the D.C. area after my Master's degree. But I wanted to keep going (In case you haven't figured it out already, I really love this stuff!). Again, Hus was apprehensive. When I was accepted to Purdue University (one of the top Communication programs in the country), he knew that we had to go. We talked about the pros and cons of this next big decision in our life. A few conversations later, Hus was on board. We packed up and moved 12 hours north to yet another small city: Lafayette, Indiana (making us a mere 10 hours away from our families and friends). Although we were closer than before, it was still a **long** drive whenever we headed back East. But, Hus was supportive. Don't get me wrong, Hus would definitely complain from time to time, but overall, I always knew that he had my back and that he was happy about the decision that we made *together*.

Decisions like these are tough. Whenever something has the ability to cause friction in your relationship or significantly change your life together, it's not going to be easy. And believe me; they will happen many times during your shared life. Whether your partner wants to change careers, start a career, open a business, work less hours, work more hours, become a stay-at-home parent, stop being a stay-at-home parent, go to school, quit school, buy a car, buy a house, move to another city, or have a baby, supporting him or her during these difficult times of decision is important.

This is not to say that you should just blindly follow. You still want to discuss all of the options available before a decision is made and you want to voice your opinion about the matter. During your discussion, you could determine when the change will occur and if and how the change will impact you, your relationship, your finances, your location, and your future. Will you need to relocate for this change? Will you need to use your savings or sell your house, car, or other possessions to pay for this change? How much stress are the two of you expecting to experience as a result of this change? How do you both plan to deal with this stress? Answering these questions, and others, will help you work through the issue.

It's perfectly acceptable for you to voice your opposition, but if this is something that will make your mate happy, you need to decide if going against the grain is really worth it. For instance, if you don't support your husband's desire to start a new career, he could build up some serious resentment towards you that could last for months, years, or even decades. Likewise, if your wife is unhappy and this new idea of hers will help alleviate some of that misery (even if you don't fully agree with her proposal), supporting her may be the path that you need to take. If after your discussion, you realize that your partner really wants whatever it is that is being proposed *and* it's a relatively reasonable idea, support for your partner may be warranted. To help you provide the best support during times of decision, follow these do's and don'ts below.

Do's and Don'ts to Supporting Your Mate's Decisions

DON'T force your ideas on your mate. Remember, this is *your partner's* aspiration. They wouldn't be bringing this discussion to the table if it weren't important to them. It's okay to voice your opinions, but you still want to support them by remaining positive and encouraging the attainment of their goals.

DON'T talk negatively about your partner's decision after the decision has been made. This will make your partner feel terrible. Even if your mate realizes that the decision was a bad idea, talking negatively about it will make them feel completely responsible for any adverse consequences you experience. I can promise that you do not want them to feel that kind of regret or remorse about the situation.

DON'T belittle your partner's ideas. Your partner is bringing these things up to you because he or she thinks that they are good ideas. Telling your mate that the plan is stupid, ridiculous, or ill-conceived is not the mature, supportive route to take.

DO consider bargaining. Sometimes, there may be room for some kind of trade-off. For instance, when Hus and I were discussing the big move to Indiana for my Ph.D., we agreed that when my time at Purdue was over, we would move back to the east coast. And, we did. Coming to a middle ground about the issue can help both sides get what they want.

DO create a list of pros and cons. Weighing the rewards and the costs associated with your partner's big plans can sometimes help you and your mate realize the practicality of this proposition.

DO evaluate the outcome of this decision. Like I said, you want to talk about all possible end results. Think about things that could go wrong and discuss ways that the two of you will address these problems if and when they occur. It's really important to anticipate any and all setbacks that may or may not transpire. And, determining what you would do when faced with these issues is a significant part of this process. What if your partner changes career paths and you can no longer pay your mortgage? Are both of you willing to downsize your home so that one of you can follow your dreams?

Mindlessly supporting your partner is not healthy for your relationship. Instead, thoroughly discuss the issue, come to a decision together, and encourage the accomplishment of these goals. This will allow your mate to feel loved and supported by you, subsequently enhancing your relationship satisfaction.

THOSE TIMES IN BETWEEN

When you're not busy supporting your wife while she's suffering from losing her job or supporting your husband when he wants to become an airline pilot at the ripe old age of 47, you still need to have your partner's back during all of those times in between. Whenever they're in trouble, arguing with a friend, complaining about work, parenting your children, or in a disagreement with *your* mother, make an effort to stand by them. This also includes sticking up for them when other people offend, harass, anger, or sadden them.

So many times we feel the need to disagree or outwardly argue against our partners to prove a point. Or, we fail to respond when someone else says or does something that impacts our partners in a negative way. When this becomes a habit, our relationships can be put on the fast track to a break-up or divorce. Being on your partner's side and having their back about certain issues, especially in front of other people, exhibits your unity and cohesiveness as a couple.

Just like anything, you don't want to always agree about every little thing to avoid causing a rift between the two of you. And, you don't need to get into physical altercations when someone offends your partner at dinner. Constructive conflict is a big part of any healthy relationship (as you will read about in chapter ten- go on, skip ahead if you want). It's okay to disagree with your mate, but taking the side of someone who is not your partner, even if you think that your mate is likely in the wrong, is a sure-fire strategy to push them away and divide the two of you. Think about those times when your best friend and your boyfriend got into an argument or your mother and your wife disagreed about something. What did you do? How did it turn out?

I can recall many instances in our relationship where Hus and I did not play on the same team. Whether I was sticking up for Hus' best friend instead of him (sorry Hus) or Hus was validating his mom's opinion over mine (it's okay, I forgive you), we've had our fair share of disagreements on this subject.

About halfway through our first ten years together, I became completely aware of the fact that I had to change the way I supported Hus. You see, Hus has been known to grumble from time to time about his friends. Maybe one friend didn't call him back when he clearly said that he would or another friend disagreed with him about something in a demeaning manner. Whatever the situation was, I regrettably had a habit of defending his friends and unknowingly disparaging Hus.

Hus would complain about his friend, I would say that his friend probably didn't mean for him to feel that way, and then I would encourage Hus to "get over it" or to "not be so sensitive." Somehow, I thought that I was making Hus feel better. I thought that I was enabling him to become a more positive person and to look at people (i.e. his friends) as good-intentioned.

Instead, I was belittling his feelings, attacking his perspective, and causing him to feel very alone. Not only did he not believe me (causing him to still view his friend poorly), but he also felt like no one understood him. And this was completely reasonable. The one person who was supposed to understand him better than anyone else (i.e. me!) was telling him that his feelings were baseless and even ridiculous. I was inadvertently criticizing him and making him feel worse than he did before we spoke. I was not playing on his team.

I would play on Hus' team most of the time, but I just wouldn't show up to games that were against his friends' teams.

The months that followed my realization turned into years. Then, our relationship became a marriage. This is where I really began to reflect upon our past interactions and understand the importance of playing on the same team.

As we do with most things, Hus and I had several conversations about how my remarks made him feel. I listened to what he had to say. I *really* listened. I tried to put myself in Hus' position. How would I feel if

Hus said those things to me? I had to take a step back and think about what I had done and maybe more importantly, what I was going to do to remedy this situation.

Hus and I decided that he was going to work harder to see the good in other people and I was going to work harder to empathize with Hus and not tell him what he should or should not do (unless he asks, of course). Just knowing how he felt helped me change my communication style about this topic and it has definitely brought us closer as a couple.

The even better news was that Hus and I were on *a team*, together. And since that day, we have both shown up to every single game; no matter who we're playing against.

What have we learned? Over the years, we've both realized that **we are on a team together** and that team members support one another, no matter what happens. Not supporting one another during these times doesn't help our relationship. In fact, it *severely* damages it. It has made each of us feel unloved, abandoned, and alone.

♥

Learning how to support one another can be a daunting task that many of us either never learn or forget to put into practice. Pay close attention to the cues sent by your partner. Determine what they need from you and try to accommodate in a sensitive, person-centered way.

Being in-tune with how our partners feel and helping them in times of distress, standing by them in times of decision, and playing on their team during all of those times in between can easily enhance feelings of closeness, intimacy, and satisfaction in our relationships.

CHAPTER two: generate some blushing

F lattery is one of the best ways to make someone feel special; particularly the one you love. Telling our partners that we like what they've done, how they look, or what they've said affirms their sense of self-worth.

Sometimes, when we see our partners day-in and day-out, we may forget to tell them that they look beautiful or that they're great at doing whatever it is that they do so well. This lack of complimenting can cause our partners to feel self-conscious about their abilities or maybe even feel like they are useless from time to time. Think about it. If you (the one person who is supposed to like your partner more than anyone else) don't think that your partner is great, who else will? And, if you never tell your partner that you love his hair or that you think she's really good at math, how will he or she ever know how you feel?

Make an effort to pay tribute to your partner on a daily basis. It can be about anything. You could tell your boyfriend that he is an excellent cook when he makes a delicious dinner or tell your wife that she looks stunning on a Tuesday afternoon or tell your mate that he is an amazing comforter when he helps you get through a tough time. How ever you decide to do it, showering your partner with flattery without going overboard (you don't need to tell your mate that he's superb at tying his shoes or that she's a dynamite fork-holder) can easily boost his or her self-esteem and overall happiness.

BENEFITS OF COMPLIMENTS

Both men and women report that they highly value compliments in their romantic relationships.[8] Many researchers[9] have even claimed that complimenting can significantly add to the intimacy and relationship satisfaction that you experience with your partner. When your mate compliments you, you feel loved and valued, which can intensify the bond that the two of you share. Drs. Eve-Ann Doohan, Ph.D., and Valerie Manusov, Ph.D., of the University of Washington, have concluded that if you're satisfied with the complimenting that is occurring in your relationship, you're also more likely to be satisfied with your relationship as a whole.[10]

And for those of you who are involved in a relationship where one person has low self-esteem, compliments can have a significant, positive impact on the connection that you share with your mate. You see, individuals with lower self-esteem tend to underestimate how much their partners love and care for them, even though research shows that individuals with low self-esteem are loved just as much by their partners as individuals with high self-esteem are loved by their partners.[11] Psychologists at the University of Waterloo (Drs. Denise Marigold, Ph.D., John Holmes, Ph.D., and Michael Ross, Ph.D.)[12] conducted three studies to investigate how low self-esteem individuals could increase their own relationship satisfaction and feelings of relationship security after receiving compliments from their partners. After an extensive review of past literature, the researchers decided that in order for low self-esteem individuals to truly "believe" the compliments given to them by their partners (because remember, low self-esteem individuals tend to not believe that their partners love them as much as they actually do), they had to reframe how they viewed and understood the compliment. And, it worked. In general, the researchers had some low self-esteem individuals discuss a compliment from their partner more concretely ("Describe exactly what your partner said to you. Include any details you can recall about where you two were at the time, what you were doing, what you were both wearing, etc.") and had other low self-esteem individuals discuss a compliment from their partner more abstractly ("Explain why your partner admired you. Describe what it meant to you and its significance to you relationship."). They also examined individuals with high self-esteem and had them do the same thing. Results showed that individuals with low self-esteem benefited from describing the meaning and significance of the compliment as opposed to describing every little detail. In particular, low self-esteem individuals "can reframe affirmations from their partners to be as meaningful as [high self-esteem individuals] generally believe them to be and, consequently, can feel just as secure and satisfied with their romantic relationships."[13]

In sum, when low self-esteem individuals receive compliments from their mates, they tend to brush them off as their partners "just being nice," "not telling them the whole truth," or even "fibbing to make them feel good." But, when these same individuals are asked to think more deeply about the meaning and intention behind the compliment, they feel more loved and secure and they actually value their relationships more than when they don't engage in any reflection about the praise.

Complimenting is not just useful for enhancing *intimacy*, *security*, and *satisfaction* in your relationship. Moderate complimenting (i.e. complimenting without going overboard) has also been shown to be an effective strategy to elicit *liking* from others,[14] including your partner. We like people who compliment us; no big shock here. And, individuals who are moderate complimenters tend to be perceived as *more attractive* than those who give too few or too many accolades.[15]

> "I love it when my wife compliments me about my contribution to the family. She'll say, 'You work so hard to make sure that we have what we need. I love that about you.' It makes me feel appreciated and loved. I would be lost without her."
>
> -Anderson, in a relationship with Christina since March 1995 and married since May 1999

But! Be careful about what you say to your partner in front of other people. Research conducted by a group of my undergraduates (Amy Remmer, Ariana Shirzadi, Julie Greenberg, and Christina Vaughn) at James Madison University[16] found that a compliment about an intimate topic* is viewed more negatively when written on a partner's public Facebook wall then when that same personal compliment is delivered via private Facebook message. Non-intimate compliments, on the other hand, are viewed positively when publicly displayed or received privately. Next time you think about complimenting your mate in front of others, whether it's on Facebook or in person, engage in some contemplation first and ask yourself these questions: Is this compliment inappropriate for this social situation? Could my partner possibly be embarrassed by this compliment? If you answered "No" to both of these questions, compliment away.

"My husband really cares about his family and friends. He would do anything for them. But they don't realize how lucky they are and they don't thank him enough. So I like to compliment him by telling him how great of a person he is, which seems to help when he doesn't feel acknowledged by them."

-Laurie, in a relationship with Gary since October 1982 and married since December 1984

CONSTRUCTING A SUPERB COMPLIMENT

Interestingly, research has shown that two-thirds of all compliments include the adjectives *nice, pretty, beautiful, good,* or *great,* and 90% of compliments include the verbs *like* or *love.*[17] Go against the grain and try to be more original by using other adjectives such as *lovely, outstanding, magnificent, gorgeous, amazing, delightful, superb, marvelous,* or *impressive* and other verbs like *admire, respect, enjoy,* or *adore.* Using these unique words will help your compliments stand out from the rest. Follow these "do's" and "don'ts" of complimenting with the most important person in your life.

---

* In their study, the intimate compliment read: "Sex was great last night. You're amazing!" And the non-intimate compliment read, "Dinner was great last night. You're amazing!"

Complimenting Do's and Don'ts

DO compliment daily. **DON'T** overdo it by complimenting about anything and everything. When you do this, your praises may seem less genuine.

DO use more unique adjectives & verbs in your tributes. **DON'T** forget about some of the more common terms. Sometimes speaking in an idiosyncratic way all of the time can cause people to view you as pompous.

DO act enthusiastic when complimenting. **DON'T** go overboard. This could make your accolades sound like sarcasm.

DO compliment about things your mate has chosen. **DON'T** *always* mention things your mate cannot change. So, instead of saying, "You have great eyes," you could say, "You're an amazing dancer." To become a great dancer, one generally has to put in a lot of time and effort. Complimenting someone on a skill is much better than complimenting someone on his or her physical beauty. Compliments about beauty should not be avoided completely; they just should not be the *only* type of compliment that you ever give your partner.

DO compliment about specific things- "I really liked the way you handled the situation with your mom. You were so calm, cool, and collected when she was being unreasonable." **DON'T** be so general that you're not personal- "You're great." Tell your partner *why* he or she is great.

DO compliment in front of others. **DON'T** compliment about personal or sensitive matters in front of others. For example, it would be completely inappropriate to praise your partner's love-making skills in front of your mom.

Complimenting has been a common topic of debate in my own marriage, with Hus and I going back and forth about who compliments too much or too little. Specifically, I tend to believe that Hus is an excessive complimenter while Hus claims that I... well... don't compliment often enough. Hus' over the top complimenting can be a bit overwhelming and has even made me feel stifled at times. In my experience, there's a fine line between sufficient and excessive complimenting. When Hus dishes out 15 or so compliments in a single day, it can get a little excessive. And, as I previously mentioned, it's not always about the *amount* of complimenting an individual dishes out. Complimenting can also feel excessive when individuals are being complimented about every little thing they do in the day or about the same thing over and over and over again. Hus can sometimes be guilty of both of these kinds of excessive complimenting.

I know, I know, what the hell am I bitching about? So many people would *love* to be complimented all of the time. I understand that, but I guess that instead of his abundant flattery making me feel good (which I know is his true intention), it sort of makes me feel bad. Why? Well, I'm not the best at throwing out compliments myself. And when Hus compliments me and I don't compliment him, I feel like an inconsiderate person. This feeling usually makes me say things like, "don't say that" or "oh, c'mon" whenever Hus praises me. Subsequently, it's not uncommon for some sort of argument to ensue after these interactions. I know what you're thinking; it's ridiculous. I agree.

My partner is very good about telling me that I look nice when he knows I went out of my way to look good or if I did something different. It's comforting to know that he's paying attention to my self-esteem issues and always tries to make me feel good about myself.

-April, in a relationship with Mike since August 2007

Sadly, *even more* conflict can develop between the two of us when we discuss my lack of complimenting. It's not that I don't compliment because there's nothing to compliment about- Hus is an amazingly supportive, understanding, loving husband- I guess I just don't think about it very often. A while back, Hus let me know that my lack of complimenting made him feel underappreciated and even unloved at times and I told him about my feelings of inadequacy and being suffocated when he went overboard with his complimenting. The good news is that we're both actively working towards adjusting our flattery so that each of us feels valued, respected, and recognized. He's tried to limit his complimenting to more significant actions of mine and I've decided to not only pay more attention to Hus' behaviors, but to also let him know when I'm grateful for having him in my life- which is definitely on a daily basis.

Once you find a nice balance between complimenting enough and not overdoing it, you'll be happy to know that you can easily elicit some warm-and-fuzzy feelings in your relationship just by letting your partner know that you think he or she is incredibly fabulous. And, as an added bonus, it can make you look more appealing in the process. The next time that the person you love does something outstanding, or even mildly magnificent for that matter, let that person know by throwing a compliment his/her way. Need help creating some praises? Here are four popular compliment topics to get you started.

4 Compliment Topics

Compliments about Attributes
"You are hilarious!"
"You're incredibly thoughtful."
"I adore your honesty."

Compliments about Appearance & Attire
"You have the most beautiful curly hair.'"
"You are gorgeous."
"That suit makes you look so professional."

Compliments about Abilities
"You're really good at basketball."
"I like the way you comfort me."
"Your organizational skills astound me."

Compliments about Actions
"It was really nice that you picked up your sister."
"It was so generous of you to donate that food."
"You work so hard to achieve your goals."

(Categories adapted from Doohan & Manusov, 2004)

♥

Showing appreciation for your partner's appealing personality, praiseworthy behaviors, and admirable accomplishments is an excellent way to maintain and intensify your relationship. It makes your mate feel valued and it can also increase perceptions of your own attractiveness. But be careful- too much complimenting could have a negative impact on your relationship. There is no need to praise your partner about every little thing. Make your compliments specific, often, and unique to increase the intimacy, closeness, and satisfaction in your relationship.

C ommunication is vital to the initiation, development, and maintenance of close relationships.[18] In fact, many researchers[19] have argued that without communication, relationships would not only fail to develop, but would cease to exist in the first place. Whether you're talking about your deepest darkest secrets or about your opinions of the latest *American Idol* contestants, communicating with your partner is important.

Researchers have examined both ends of this chitchat continuum and discovered that it's just as important to discuss mundane, everyday topics with your partner, as it is to delve into your innermost beliefs, values, and attitudes with the one you love.

TALK ABOUT YOUR EXPERIENCES

Talking and listening to each other about the day's ups and downs has been shown to have a significant impact on the positive emotions and feelings of closeness you share in your relationship.[20]

Hus and I definitely subscribe to this belief. Hus usually gets home from work after I do. *Before* we had children, we had a pretty consistent after-work routine. And it went a little something like this: First, I used to always work in my office upstairs until our dogs began to bark uncontrollably. What do I mean by uncontrollable? Let's just say that we used to have three dogs that were rather difficult to manage. I would then go downstairs to greet Hus and give him a kiss hello. He would go to the kitchen, take his shoes off, get a drink, and then we would both walk back upstairs. Since Hus' job required (and still requires) that he get dirty (I have a seriously hard-working man), he always took (and still takes) a shower before dinner. And while he showered, I would sit in the bathroom and we would each talk about the significant, and not-so-significant, events of our day. I'm serious; we did this almost every single night for many years. We would talk about the good, the bad, and the ugly. Then we would go back downstairs, I would usually make dinner, and we would continue our conversation while we ate together and watched a few of our favorite shows before bed. Since we've had twins, some proverbial wrenches are constantly being thrown into this routine. But, no matter what is going on, we still take time out of every single night to review our days together.

"Communication is the key to happiness in any marriage. Without constant and clear conversation, couples can begin to grow apart. The simple acts of speaking and listening demonstrate a real interest in your partner."

-Samantha, in a relationship with Steve since December 2001 & Married since August 2007

I've always really enjoyed these nightly conversations with Hus, and a few years ago, I read an interesting journal article that has further solidified my opinion of the importance of this rather simple communication activity. Drs. Angela Hicks, Ph.D., and Lisa Diamond, Ph.D., psychology professors at Westminster College and University of Utah respectively, published a study[21] in *Personal Relationships* that examined the impact that disclosing day-to-day activities has on your daily feelings and emotions.

Participants in this study included 48 married or cohabitating heterosexual couples (so, a total of 96 people), all of who had been together for more than two years. Each individual within each couple was given a diary to write in at the end of every day for 21 days. Each day, the participants were asked to write down, describe, and evaluate their most positive experience and their most stressful or bothersome experience of that day. They were also asked to indicate whether or not they disclosed the event to their partner that day. Lastly, they completed a survey that assessed their positive and negative emotions during each day of the study.

The research findings here were quite interesting. First, telling *and* being told about positive events were significantly associated with positive feelings at the end of the day for both men and women. I know what you're thinking: the participants were likely happier because they experienced positive events during their day, not because they talked about them. This was not so. Individuals who *did not* disclose their positive experiences with their mates reported less positive emotions at the end of their day than individuals who *did* discuss their positive experiences with their partners. So, it wasn't about whether people experienced positive events or not (each person had at least one positive event each day), it was about whether they told their significant other about those events that mattered most when it came down to their emotions.

What does all of this mean? Talking to your mate about the positive aspects of his or her day is more than just small talk; it's an important conversation that you should engage in to increase positive emotions in yourself *and* in your mate. Whether you're a college student in your first serious relationship, a twenty-something hoping that he's "the one," happily married with a few energetic children, or an empty-nester enjoying a quite house again, according to Drs. Hicks and Diamond, asking your partner about his or her day may lead to increased feelings of happiness, closeness, and intimacy in your relationship. And these advantages are not just limited to your end-of-day discussions. All of those other little chats through out the day count, too.

> "We go on long walks as much as possible and talk about everything on our minds. We talk through problems, concerns, worries, and all the good stuff, too. By the time we get home from the walk, we've gotten a bit of exercise, had some free therapy, and know what page the other one is on a whole lot more clearly than we did before we left."
>
> -Kersten, in a relationship with Anthony since 1998 & married since 2000

TALK ABOUT YOURSELF

Okay, you know that the ordinary, day-to-day talk is beneficial to your relationship, but what about those deep, intimate conversations? Aren't those important, too? YES! It's crucial that you and your partner share your personal beliefs, opinions, attitudes, thoughts, feelings, wants, needs, and goals with one another. I know: that's a lot of talking! But communication is key to any relationship (it's not just a cliché), whether you're just starting out or have been together for a few decades.

> "John has shared his passions of philosophy, martial arts, and the Detroit Pistons with me. In return, I've introduced him to my passions of cooking, dancing, and my cultural heritage with him. Learning about each other's passions has helped us grow as individuals and as a couple."
>
> -Lisa, in a relationship with John since 2008 & married since May 2011

A great way to develop new relationships or further enhance your current relationship is to engage in reciprocal self-disclosure. Self-disclosure has been defined by researchers as the process of revealing information about yourself to others.[22] This can come in the form of expressing your opinions about certain political issues, discussing your hobbies, uncovering your values and beliefs, or divulging your life dreams. The information that is disclosed can be new (information that your partner does not already know about) or it can be information about yourself that has already been expressed in the past. When you're self-disclosing, you're not just revealing the information that's actually in your message. You're also allowing people to make inferences about you based on what you say. For instance, if you tell your boyfriend that you like to scrapbook, he might infer that you also like doing other crafty things like making homemade greeting cards, decorating your house, or cooking gourmet meals.

While research has shown that self-disclosure has the ability to ignite feelings of intimacy and closeness and improve relationship satisfaction,[23] you should also know that self-disclosing does not always result in positive outcomes. We tend to only experience the aforementioned benefits when our disclosures don't offend, embarrass, or hurt the feelings of one or both individuals involved. In general, it's good to follow the following 6 guidelines when revealing information about yourself to someone else.

6 Guidelines for Self-Disclosing

Reserve your most important disclosures for significant, ongoing relationships. Don't just tell anyone that you like to watch porn every Tuesday night. You might want to save that one for someone you feel *really* close to.

Make sure that disclosures are appropriate to the topic at hand and fit the flow of the conversation. You want to reduce anxiety in interactions with your partner, not cause it (especially when this person is a new partner). If your new boyfriend is talking about where he's from, it's probably not the best time to mention your pesky drug habit. Or, if your wife is discussing her thoughts on the latest hot-button political issue of the day, you probably shouldn't bring up your amazing ability to hula-hoop. Both of these topics do not fit or connect with what your partner was saying. It could not only make the conversation awkward, but also make your partner feel like you weren't listening.

Match the level and amount of the other's disclosure. Again, you don't want to create an awkward situation by disclosing something very personal about yourself when the conversation is not headed in that direction. For instance, if your conversation partner is talking about their hometown, it *would be appropriate* for the conversation to move to how many siblings you have because these two topics are at about the same level of intimateness. However, for most people, it *would not be appropriate* for the conversation about hometowns to shift towards talking about religious beliefs. In the same respect, you should try to match the other person's amount of self-disclosure. For instance, it would be inappropriate for you to disclose for 20 minutes when your partner only disclosed for 2 or 3 minutes.

Begin a relationship with safe, nonrisky disclosures. Don't disclose that you were in jail for grand theft auto when you were 20 or that you like going to swinger's clubs on a first date (or even a third or fourth date for that matter). Save this information for later. Instead, start off by revealing where you're from, where you went to high school or college, or what your hobbies are.

Remember that style of disclosure is as important as substance. Be conscious of your paralanguage (i.e. the way that you talk) and other nonverbal behaviors. The *way* you say something can influence your message. So, think about your tone, pitch, rate, use of sarcasm, facial expressions, and body gestures when self-disclosing. For example, using sarcasm when disclosing information about yourself can make you appear insincere.

Disclose in small doses. There are two parts to this guideline. First, don't disclose everything about yourself all at once. Like I mentioned earlier, save some stuff for later. Second, don't monopolize the conversation. Let the other person disclose some information, too. The second part to this guideline is important for couples just starting out *and* for couples who have been around the block a few times. Controlling the conversation- about anything- is never a good communication habit to have.

Guidelines adapted from Trenholm & Jensen's (2008) book entitled, *Interpersonal Communication*.

It's important to note that although these rules are great for anyone who is disclosing information to a relationship partner, they are more important to follow when you're in a new or developing relationship than when you are in a long-term, established relationship. This is because individuals who have extensive interactions with one another tend to also have a certain comfort level, and maybe even an insider language, that younger relationships lack. Saying that, it's still important to keep these rules in mind *whenever* you decide to disclose any information about yourself to another person. So, express your feelings, thoughts, wants, and needs to your partner while offering up some empathy and understanding when they do the same.

TALK ABOUT
YOUR RELATIONSHIP

Talking about day-to-day happenings and sharing your inner most thoughts and feelings with your significant other are both extremely important to the success of your relationship. And in addition to those conversations, you want to also periodically "check-up" with one another about your own relationship-- where it stands, how it's working out for both of you, and where it's going. You want to communicate about your relationship *and* about the status of the communication in your relationship.

Talking to your partner about these things, while it may be difficult at times, will hopefully save your relationship from the dissatisfaction plague by nipping any concerns that you have in the bud. Then, if you're actually able to have effective conversations about these concerns before they become out-of-control relationship issues, you will not only become more satisfied in your relationship and in your relationship's communication, but your relationship will likely be strengthened in the process.

Everyone always wants to know where their relationship stands and maybe more importantly, where it's going. So many times, partners are not on the same page here. One partner may have very strong feelings and thoughts of marriage, while the other partner is ready to hit the road in a few months. For many people, it's scary to openly and honestly discuss this with their mate. For those individuals, they could turn to testing the waters by enacting one (or more) of the seven "secret tests" identified by Drs. Leslie Baxter, Ph.D., and William Wilmot, Ph.D., two very well-known scholars in the field of interpersonal communication, to seek information about the state of their relationships.[24]

The first type of test is known as an **endurance test.** This occurs when an individual increases the costs of the relationship to see if the other person stays or leaves. For instance, Jill may know that Friday night is Jack's poker night, but she decides to tell him that taking her out on a date that night instead of playing poker would make her really happy. Jack's response would give Jill insight into how far Jack would go for their relationship (i.e. her happiness). This type of test can tell you a lot about your relationship, but be careful; creating a ridiculous endurance test or too many endurance tests may make your partner feel like you're very needy and controlling.

Second, you could use an ***indirect suggestion.*** Here, you would hint or joke about the status of your relationship to see what your partner says. For instance, Jack might joke about loving Jill just to see if she reciprocates by saying that she loves him too. If your partner responds unfavorably, then you can brush it off as a joke. No big deal, right?

The third test is called **public presentation** and is where one person introduces their partner to other people as their boyfriend or girlfriend to see how their partner reacts. While this test is very effective, it requires some courage since you'll be in front of other people. Everyone, including yourself, will be able to see your partner's reaction. So, if it's a bad one, you may be embarrassed.

In the fourth type of test, known as the **triangle test**, individuals decide to go out with another person (who is not their partner) to see if their partner gets jealous or individuals may tell their partner that they think someone else is attractive to see their reaction. This test is very dangerous (and rather disrespectful) because some people may be so consumed with jealousy that they end the relationship right then and there.

Fifth, you could also initiate a **separation test**. Here, Jill would tell Jack that she didn't want to see him for a certain amount of time to see if she misses him. You know this one. It could be as simple as not seeing each other for a couple of nights when you're used to hanging out every day or as serious going on "a break" for a few weeks.

The sixth secret test is called a **third party test.** This is where you ask your friends and family their opinions about the relationship. This can be very insightful. It's often difficult to take a step back and evaluate your relationship when you're deeply involved. Asking people who you trust and care about is a great way to determine where your relationship stands and if it's on the right track; or on the right track according to your friends.

Lastly, you could utilize a **direct test** to gain valuable information about your relationship. Here, you would flat-out ask your partner a direct question about your relationship. For instance, Jack might ask Jill, "Where do you see this relationship in a month?" or "Do you still love me?" or "Are you planning to move out?" Using this type of test is effective because an individual usually finds out exactly what they want to know, but this kind of directness may make a relationship partner feel uncomfortable or even pressured to respond in a certain way, which could be detrimental to the overall relationship; so be careful.

All of these communication tests help people seek information about their developing relationships. When the "answers" to these tests are favorable, relationships tend to intensify more quickly than when responses are less favorable. It is also important to note that some of these tests may never be used in a relationship. Instead, you may decide to use a *direct test* and then never feel the urge to use any of the other tests. Or, you may use all of these tests to gain that vital information needed to evaluate your relationship. Whatever you do, testing the waters is an important process in any relationship.

TALK ABOUT MARRIAGE

Unfortunately, marriages these days still only have about a 50% success rate. A lot (but certainly not all) of the problems associated with divorce tend to stem from a lack of communication about the inner-workings of marriage *before* those papers are signed. Many people get into marriage thinking that their love for each other will fix any and all problems they may encounter in the future. Well I'm sorry to say this, but love won't pay the bills, love won't do the dishes or cut the grass, and love won't change your partner's mind about children. Talking about these three important topics below *before* you get hitched (and continuing the conversation through out your entire marriage) has the potential to alleviate the intensity and/or number of arguments you most definitely will experience as a married couple.

MONEY

As noted by Dr. Jan Andersen, Ph.D., an Associate Professor Emeritus of Family and Consumer Sciences at California State University, Sacramento, although financial problems are not usually listed in the *top five* reasons for divorce, they can easily cause some serious issues and conflict in any marriage.[25] While talking about money can't solve the problems associated with a small wallet, it can allow you and your partner to understand each other better when it comes to your piggy bank.

Before getting married, you and your mate should openly discuss any and all

"My boyfriend and I, who are both struggling financially, talk about our finances from time to time and try to come up with plans to make things better. We also try to pick up each other's slack when one of us can afford it more than the other. I know that once we get through this rough patch, things will be better again. Talking about it really helps."

-Heather, in a relationship with Justin since May 2008

debts you each have (this includes student loans, car leans, mortgages, credit card debt, etc.), you and your partner's spending and saving habits (even if you don't have any), and each of your yearly incomes. Not only do you need to talk about how much money you make, spend, and save, but you should also discuss how you plan to pay off your debt. Will all of the debt go into one "debt pile" and then both of you will pay it off together? Or, will you each continue to pay off your own individual debts? Further, it's especially critical to consider your plans for sharing money. Will you have separate bank accounts or one joint account? Or, will you have two separate accounts *and* a shared account? How will the bills be paid? Who will be responsible for paying them? How will you determine what counts as a "necessary bill" and what counts as an "unnecessary bill"? What will you do with the "unnecessary bills"? For instance, is your boyfriend's monthly subscription to *Maxim Magazine* something you both want to continue paying after marriage?

In addition, it's important to talk about the different values you each place on money. Do you need the latest and greatest gadgets or can you do without? Maybe even more important, do you think that *your mate* should do without? Do you think that it's perfectly acceptable to spend $100 on a pair of jeans or does that bother you? Figuring out all of this stuff before you say "I do" (and then continuing to discuss it after your nuptials) can really help you start your marriage on the right foot. And, if you discover major problems during this discussion, problems that can't be solved or ignored, you may need to end this relationship and call it quits. I know that sounds harsh, but money problems have ruined a significant number of marriages, so discussing this issue prior to sealing the deal could help you avoid some heartache.

Growing up, my mom used to tell me a lot of stories about the first year of her marriage to my dad. And there was one story that stood out to me. My mom and dad started dating when my mom was a teenager and my dad was 7.5 years older than her. She said that he always impressed her. "He would walk around with a big wad of cash in his pocket and pay for everything we did together. And we did a lot of stuff. He never hesitated about buying anything. He also always had a hot rod and would always brag about everything he did to modify it. I thought he was rich!"

Then, my naïve 19-year-old mom married my 27-year-old dad. Four months in, they decided that my mom should take over the finances and organize the bills. She didn't think anything of it; until she sat down at their kitchen table. As she says, "I sat there, looked at "our" situation, and was in complete shock. He didn't even have a bank account! That "wad of cash" was it! It was a very unsettling moment for me." My mom was realizing that my dad wasn't rich at all. He made very little money, carried all of that money around in his pocket, and didn't have a dime in savings.

My mom cried. She couldn't believe what she was seeing. They had **never** talked about money when they were dating. She had no idea how much money he made or how much debt he had. She also didn't realize that when they got married, all of "her" money and all of "his" money was going to become "their" money. She was going to share his debt, share his bills, and therefore, share in **all** of his financial troubles.

She would say to me, "We ate hotdogs and pancakes for the first three years of our marriage! If you don't want to be surprised like I was, you need to talk about these things **before** you sign those papers!"

To help get the conversation going, you and your partner could separately write down your attitudes about money and how much you value it. Then, you could each make a list of questions (p.s. you can include some of the questions mentioned above) that you'd like to go over.

DIVISION OF LABOR

Dirty dishes, cars that won't start, smelly laundry, and long grass. We've all encountered these things in our lives. And before you get hitched, you have to deal with these problems all by yourself. And, it would make sense that your responsibilities would be cut in half when you get married, right? Regrettably, many couples have one person who does the majority of the chores. Before you wed, talk to your partner about who they expect to do the household chores. While the chores don't have to be perfectly divided down the middle (wouldn't that be great if they were though?), it's really important that you and your mate are on the same page about who should do each task. So, if you both agree that you should do everything, and you're both completely okay with that, then good. But, if you don't want to do it all, then now is the time to voice your opinion and creatively divide things.

If you're already married and you feel like your partner is not pulling their weight, then you may need to have a talk. The purpose of this conversation is really meant to *discuss expectations* so that you can determine if you like what you hear and decide if you will be happy down the road.

Here are some tasks you and your mate could talk about divvying up: taking out the trash, doing the dishes, cutting the grass/gardening, loading and folding laundry (and putting it away!), dusting and polishing, sweeping and vacuuming, cleaning bathrooms, cleaning the fridge, mopping the floors, dealing with car troubles/appliance breakdowns/etc., organizing and paying the bills, scheduling things (like doctor appointments), making dinner, maintaining the sanity, and anything else you can think of. You will be much more satisfied in your relationship if and when you two can come to a consensus or even a compromise about how to deal with dividing labor before the big day.

Hus and I lived together for 3 years before we got hitched, so we had some time to figure out all of the household duty nonsense. If I remember correctly, I think we started off by just picking chores. Surprisingly, our individual to-do lists were just about the same size. For example, I decided to do the dishes and Hus would do the laundry, I would organize the bills and Hus would handle the cars (taxes, titling, oil changes, repairs, etc.), I decided to take our dogs (we had three at the time) to their groomer and vet appointments and Hus decided to take out the trash. Wow! I couldn't believe it was that easy!

My own dad didn't do much around the house. And even if he did randomly switch the laundry or load the dishwasher, he didn't have any chores that he consistently completed on a daily (or even weekly) basis. Hell, I think the child-version of myself did more chores than my dad. So when Hus said he was willing to take care of half of our household tasks, I was ecstatic. I wanted to pinch myself to see if it was real.

Well, it *was* real. For about a month. When Hus and I first moved in together, my schedule was a lot more flexible than his (I was in graduate school and Hus was working 50-60 hours a week). And after some time, his busy schedule resulted in me doing most of the day-to-day tasks. After a couple years of that, I was done. Hus and I needed to have that talk I mentioned earlier.

Not only did I hate doing the laundry and taking the trash out everyday, but I also didn't want to become "the wife" (in the traditional sense). I had seen *that* movie before: husband and wife both work, wife still takes care of house, wife makes dinner, wife takes care of kids, husband sits on couch, wife nags husband, husband bitches about how wife nags too much. No sir. That life was *not* for me. I wanted us to be equal partners in our relationship. I didn't want one of us to be the boss. I didn't want one of us to resent the other. I didn't want a parent-child relationship with my husband. And I knew Hus didn't want these things either.

So we talked and talked and talked. We categorized the chores into tasks that had to be completed everyday, tasks that could be done once a week, and tasks that could be done once every two weeks. We talked about which chores logically made sense for each of us to take on (based on our skills, likes, and schedules) and we agreed that we would be flexible if something ever came up and we had to switch things around. We decided that we were going to help one another out when one of us was tired or sick or out-of-town. Lastly, we both wanted to be responsible for our own chores and to not be nagged by the other partner if those chores were not completed "on time." Basically, I took a chill pill. And eventually, we came to understand each other's point of view.

But it wasn't easy and it didn't happen overnight. In fact, it took a few more ~~arguments~~ discussions before we arrived where we are now (which still isn't perfect, by the way). We have to work at it. It's a continuous conversation.

From time to time, we'll have a "gripe session" where we talk about things that are bothering us. And household chores are a common theme. These little chats usually start with ~~me~~ one of us telling the other that we feel like we're doing too much at home. Together, we talk about what needs to change and how we can change it; even if this means that we need to switch responsibilities. For example, Hus used to be responsible for the laundry on his own. We realized that loading, switching, folding, and putting away the laundry for four people every single week was not going to get done by one person. So now, we share this chore. We do it together, every week. Okay, well maybe not *every* week. But now when the laundry doesn't get done, it's because we procrastinated *together*.

Figuring all of this stuff out is not as bad as you might think. At least with us, we have an open, respectful dialogue where we both feel comfortable talking about these things. This is partly due to our motivation for a successful marriage, but mostly it's because we both inherently want to be equal. Hus does not want to be the boss of me and I do not want to be the boss of Hus. Although I can't promise that you both will always follow through with your decisions, at least you'll know what your mate expects of you and they will know what you expect of them. And, as Hus would say, "Knowing is half the battle!"

KIDS

Here's the big one: kids. Talk about children with your partner. Do you want kids? How many do you want to have? If you're someone who really wants kids and your mate doesn't, this is a **HUGE** problem. Understand that you **will not** be able to change your partner's mind in the future. If you stay together and never have kids, you will build up resentment. If you stay together and have kids without your mate being fully on board, your mate will resent you. If this is an issue for you, break it off now. Sorry to be harsh, but this is usually a deal-breaker for most people.

You also need to talk about who is going to take care of the kids. Do you expect one person to stay home and not work, are you going to take the daycare route, or are the two of you going to split up the care giving? After you've got all of that squared away, it's important to discuss child raising. Initially, you could discuss things related to infancy like who will wake up in the middle of the night or who will be responsible for changing diapers, feeding, cleaning up, bathing, etc.? Then, you could discuss issues like how you are going to deal with discipline problems. Who is going to do homework with the kids? Who will drive your kids to and from all of their functions (school, extra-curriculars, play dates, etc.)? Talking about kids **before** marriage and answering some of these questions will help you determine if your mate is the right person for you.

The fact of the matter is that being a parent is tough. Whether it's your first child or your seventh; it's stressful. Believe me, I know- Hus and I have twins. With all of the diaper changing, holding, feeding, burping, rocking, shhhh-ing, and worrying that takes place in those first few months, your relationship with the person who created this tiny human being with you may begin to suffer. It is vital that you do not let this happen. You'll have this overwhelming desire to spend every-waking moment staring at, talking to, talking about, playing with, and caring for your new bundle of joy. But, you still need to work on your relationship with your partner-in-crime. You know, the person who got you into this mess in the first place.

Sadly, having kids can end relationships and ruin marriages. The stress from all of the new responsibilities and the hours and hours taken away from the alone time you once had with your partner can put a serious strain on even the healthiest of relationships. The best way to avoid the many issues that will most definitely arise is to not put your relationship with your significant other on the back burner. You're going to have to figure out how to use both proverbial front burners- one for your baby and one for your partner.

Hus and I always knew that we wanted children. Before we wed, we talked about kids a lot. We wanted 2-4, boys *and* girls if possible, and we wanted to give them some family names. What we failed to discuss in detail until I found out that I was pregnant (about 8 years into our relationship), was all of the new responsibilities and duties that we were going to incur after our baby was born.† We started off talking about our

---

† Hus and I did not know that we were having twins until I was 25 weeks (about 6 months) pregnant! Up until that point, we thought that we were having one baby.

feelings about diaper changing, feeding, and sleeping. Thank goodness, Hus and I both said that we didn't have a problem doing any of these things. We also talked about how we wanted our children to bond with *both* of us and that we would do anything to make sure that one of us didn't become the "helper parent." We both wanted to be fully involved with everything. We also talked about childcare- we would try our hardest to make this equal too, but we knew that my schedule was a lot more flexible than Hus'.

Then, we had twins instead of just one baby. And a lot of our detailed plans were thrown out and we were quickly hurled into let's-just-do-whatever-we-can-to-survive mode. But we still tried to be as equal as possible. Looking back over the first couple years of our life with twins, I think we've done a relatively good job.

Sure, there were times where we were both extremely frustrated and our marriage was tested. For example, during the first year of his life, our son had reflux and was very colicky. His incessant crying and need to be carried everywhere was terribly challenging. The amount of attention that he demanded was difficult for Hus and I to deal with because we didn't always agree about how to best handle the situation (and we also had a second crying baby to soothe). Coupled with the sleep deprivation that we were both experiencing, Hus and I would get into arguments about all kinds of things related to our cranky son.

"I've been carrying him around all day;
what the hell have you done?"

"You're not holding him right. If you would
hold him like *this* he would stop screaming!"

"Stop getting annoyed by him! He's just a baby!
And his stomach hurts! He can't help it!"

"What the f*#% are you doing? Shut him up!"

These phrases (and several dozen others) were said by Hus and myself many times each day. And they didn't help our marriage. We were angry at one another about things we couldn't control. It was ridiculous. The good news is that you eventually get out of this phase. The bad news is that some couples say or do things during this phase that negatively and sometimes permanently change their relationship. Before you have kids, make a list of problems you may encounter (talk to your friends who have kids) and then talk about how you will address these new stressors. Then, when you actually have young children, try not to sweat the small stuff.

I realize that all of this may a BIT overwhelming. Don't worry; you don't need to talk about these important issues in **one** conversation- that would be insane. And, these shouldn't be conversation topics for a first date (yikes!). Instead, *begin* these conversations when marriage has become a serious option for you and your partner and then spread these conversations out over the course of your serious pre-marriage relationship and maintain the discussion through out your post-wedding romance. Talking about money, division of labor, and kids prior to walking down the aisle can help you better navigate marital problems later on. And, continuing to discuss these issues as your marriage blossoms is definitely going to help you improve your ability to solve problems when they come up. Remember, love may conquer all, but it sure as hell doesn't clean the house, put your screaming kid to bed, or pay off those pesky student loans.

Keeping the lines of communication open by talking with your partner on a daily basis- about anything from a tiff you had with a coworker to your thoughts on the last season of *Lost* to your stance on Obamacare to your plans for children- is a necessary component to every healthy relationship. It may feel like you're constantly talking, but believe me, your relationship will thank you for working hard to maintain it in these difficult, yet seemingly simple conversations.

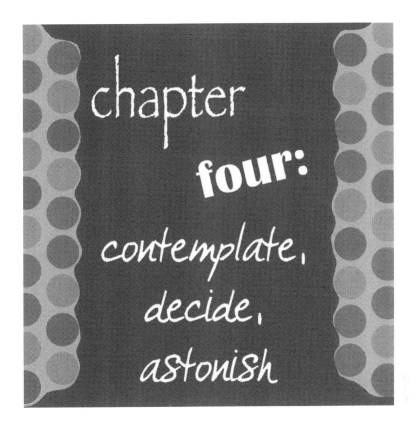

chapter four:

contemplate, decide, astonish

I don't know about you, but I *love* surprises! Big ones, small ones, shocking ones, and even the ones that I find out about beforehand; I love 'em all. And, I would venture to say that many of you love them, too. Surprises are a great way to spice things up in your relationship. And, we all know how important that is.

BE SPONTANEOUS

Surprise the one you love by doing something out of the ordinary. For instance, if making dinner is not usually your specialty, catch your partner off guard by making his or her favorite meal. You could even do something as simple as bringing home a favorite candy bar or taking the kids to a babysitter and renting a movie at home for just the two of you. Feeling like a teenager again? Go for a drive, park somewhere, and make out in the back seat. Big or small, anything you decide to do shows your significant other that you were thinking of him or her.

Not surprisingly (pun intended), researchers have found support for this idea. Specifically, studies have shown that giving others gifts can cause them to like you,[26] be instrumental in initiating new relationships,[27] and enhance already developed romances.[28]

Catching your partner off guard by doing something unique and/or presenting your mate with a little gift should not only be reserved for special occasions. A regular Tuesday afternoon is also a great time to astonish the one you love with something out of the ordinary. Try one (or a few) of these 7 romantic surprise ideas with your partner.

7 Romantic Surprises

Make a Romantic Meal
Get out the chocolate, pomegranate, vanilla ice cream and asparagus (all of which are aphrodisiacs). Set the table, light candles, play some Marvin Gaye, and surprise your partner by making them a romantic meal just for the two of you. While making a meal is great for any special occasion, it is also perfect for those just-for-the-hell-of-it surprises.

Write a Poem
Take some time out of your day and write a poem for the one you love. It can be serious, sappy, romantic, or even funny. It doesn't matter how long it is (4 lines or 4 pages)-- just write about how you feel. I know this sounds a bit cheesy, but I've written many little love poems for Hus over the last 11 years. It's nice to look at them now and remember how I felt when I wrote them, and it makes him feel special.

Jump in the Shower
Yep, you read correctly. Surprise your showering mate by jumping in and sharing some alone time. Lather up and have fun!

Give Flowers
This may sound cliché, but bringing or sending your partner flowers is a very thoughtful surprise. Whether you bring your mate a single rose on your way back from the mall, send 3 dozen lilies to their work, or pick a daisy while on a walk together, giving someone flowers never goes out of style.

Treat Your Love

Gifts don't always have to be big and extravagant to be special. Bring a little treat home to surprise your partner. Next time you're at the grocery store, buy your partner his or her favorite candy bar or bring a milkshake home the next time you're at a fast food joint. This small gesture will show your partner that you're always thinking of him or her.

Plan a Secret Vacation

This is an incredibly romantic way to surprise your partner. Whether you go down the street for a tour of your hometown and stay at a local bed-and-breakfast or travel to the Caribbean for a week-long cruise with the one you love, surprising someone with a top secret romantic get-a-way is an excellent way to intensify your relationship and express your love.

Leave a Note

Compose a brief love note for your partner and leave it in a special place. One to two sentences will do; a simple "I love you" goes a long way. Put it on the mirror in the bathroom, on the windshield of his or her car, in his or her lunch bag, or get really creative and leave notes in multiple places so that your mate will find them all day long.

Even though surprises that are completely out-of-the-blue are wonderful ways to express your love to someone, let's be honest, most of the time your mate knows when to expect a present from you. When you're in a romantic relationship, it always seems like there's an anniversary, birthday, Valentine's Day, or other present-sharing holiday right around the corner. Gift giving can be an important part of many close relationships. No pressure, but the *right* gift can show someone how much you care about him or her, while the wrong gift can make that same person wonder if you understand him or her at all.

In the beginning of our relationship, Hus (my then boyfriend) bought me a watch. It was a really nice watch- an expensive watch. But, I was young, and, I didn't (and still don't) care for expensive things, especially expensive jewelry. I'm just a bargain-hunting, knock-off-wearing, ridiculously-pricey-shit-that-I-could-find-at-Target-despising kind of girl. I thought Hus knew this. Apparently, he didn't. As I unwrapped the box and saw the *Seiko* label, I thought to myself, "What the hell is this?" About a second or two later, I had the box open. And there it was-- a bright and shiny, brand new, extravagant watch. I took off my "Oops I Did It Again" Britney Spears watch (c'mon people, it was the late 90s, the watch was bright pink, and it played her music as the alarm) and fastened the white gold, fancy-schmancy watch to my wrist.

"John is really good at surprising me with little things, some recent examples are a surprise trip to an ice cream shop during a long car ride or bringing me a cold soda when I was unpacking after our recent move. The small things remind me that we are very important to each other. My in-laws also told us early in the relationship that every year we need to take a trip alone and they would watch our kids. We just did that a week or two ago and it was amazing and definitely helped us remember why we fell in love in the first place!

-Rebecca, in a relationship with John since September 2003 & married since August 2006

Looking down at it, I felt like Hus didn't know anything about me. Did he ever listen to anything I said? If he did, it would have been obvious that I wasn't one of "those girls." I showed the watch to my best friend, and she completely agreed that it was an odd gift... for me at least. Needless to say, this was one surprise that did not go into my gift hall of fame and it did not make me feel loved.

PUT SOME THOUGHT INTO IT

Interestingly, Dr. Elizabeth Dunn, Ph.D., at the University of British Columbia along with her colleagues actually looked at how gift-giving impacts romantic relationships.[29] To examine this issue, the researchers had couples come into a lab and individually rank four gift certificates based on their own personal preferences. Next, they were asked to pick the best gift certificate for their partners. The participants were then individually told that their partners had chosen a gift certificate for them. Participants were lastly asked to evaluate the perceived similarity they had with their partners and their relationship's future potential. A little confusing?

Let me clarify with an example: Jack and Jill are dating and they decide to participate in this study. Once they arrive at the lab, Jack and Jill each rank four gift certificates based on their own preferences. Jill then picks the best one for Jack and Jack picks the best one for Jill. Jack is shown the gift certificate that Jill chose for him, and vice versa. Finally, Jack and Jill take a survey evaluating their relationship. Simple, right? Well, what made the study interesting was that the *researchers* actually chose the gift certificates for each participant based on the initial responses they each provided about their own preferences. The researchers manipulated the study so that participants were told that their partners either chose their most favorite gift certificate (which would be considered a "good" gift) or their least favorite gift certificate (which would be considered a "bad" gift).

Like many things, men and women responded very differently to this task. Men who thought they had received a "bad gift" from their partner reported less similarity with them and also stated that they thought their relationships would be shorter than men who received "good gifts" from their partners. Give a man a bad gift and it may negatively affect your relationship. Women, on the other hand, actually reported *more* similarity and *longer* projected relationship lengths when they received a "bad gift" than women who received a "good gift". I know what you're thinking. No, this does not mean that women like bad gifts. Instead, the researchers believed that women might have felt forced to think about all of the positive aspects of their relationships and their partners because the "bad gift" caused them to worry about the status of their relationships. "Are we not close enough?" While men likely felt hurt by the fact that their partners did not know them well enough to choose the gift certificate that they would have been most excited about, women probably made excuses for their partners' choices to help "save their relationship" that was so obviously failing. Clearly, the responses by both men and women are not healthy for your relationship. The take-home message: spend time getting to know your partner so that you can easily think of thoughtful gifts that he or she will absolutely love.

Okay, back to my story. Looking back, I think I *did* make some excuses for Hus when he gave me that watch. "He's never given me a bad gift before. He had good intentions. He'll do better next time." Don't worry, Hus fully redeemed himself a few gifts later. He made me a wooden trunk with our names burned into the front and notches on the back for every year we had been together. He has since added a new notch each subsequent year (there are currently eleven notches adorning the back of this treasure). Over the years, I have slowly filled this trunk with hundreds of keepsakes related to our relationship. I love that I can open it anytime, take a few things out, and reminisce about each memory inside. I adored this trunk when he gave it to me, and I love it everyday when I look at it in my office. It's one of my favorite gifts of all time. And, it's probably one of the least expensive gifts he's ever given me.

While most homemade gifts don't cost a lot of money, they can become more valuable to your partner than any Xbox, iPod, or a pair of expensive earrings. Try one of these four homemade gift ideas that you can easily make for someone you love.

"I still get fresh flowers almost weekly and we have dinner by candlelight every evening that we are both home."

- Margaret, in a relationship with Jerry since 1978 & married since 1979

4 Homemade Gift Ideas

Create a Set of Candles

Instead of spending tons of money on expensive designer candles, make your own. Go to the arts & crafts store and pick out some unscented candle wax and something to put the wax in (either a glass vase or a mold to make stand-alone candles). Then, you can choose your partner's favorite scent and color to mix in the wax (By the way, if you don't find a color that you like in the candle aisle, you can use crayons! Just drop the whole crayon in the hot wax and the color will spread through out. You can even use scented crayons to add a color and scent that you like!). Make sure that you strictly follow candle-making instructions because you don't want to ruin your pots and pans or get your candle stuck in a mold. Once your candles have hardened, there are many different ways that you can decorate them including, gluing a ribbon around the center or gluing small items to the bottom half of the candle. These candles work great for people who need to take a break, sit back, and relax. You could even include some massage oils and a "one free massage" coupon in this gift to be used with the candles. This is definitely a very romantic and thoughtful gift.

Design Some Jewelry

Stay away from Kay's, Shaw's, and Jared's this year. Instead, head off to a bead store or arts & crafts depot to collect things for your own jewelry. You could take a jewelry-making class, get a book on the subject, or look up a tutorial online to learn about making gorgeous jewelry for your mate. You could even make a custom tag with your name on it to show who the jewelry was made by. Something like, "Custom Jewelry by Jennie" on a tag attached to the jewelry would be the perfect finishing touch to this creative gift. Not only will this save you some serious mulah, but your partner will delight in all of the thought and hard work you put into making him or her custom jewelry.

A Photo Memory Book

There are a couple of different ways that you can go about doing this. First, you can go to a photo book website, upload your photos, choose a book, and then organize your photos in the book. Think of a cute title for your book and you can even include captions with the photos. Second, you could create your own photo scrapbook (you know, with paper and tape). Choose a theme for your book and include photos and captions through out. A great theme for either of these books is a "reasons for love" theme. Provide 20 (give or take a few) reasons that you love your partner. When your partner receives this gift, he or she will treasure it forever.

Paint a Painting

Are you the artistic type? Get a canvas from the arts & crafts store, choose some paint colors, and create a meaningful painting for the one you love. From a modern geometrical design that matches your partner's home decor to the scene of your first date to an interpretation of what love means to you, painting something for your mate is an intimate way to express yourself and show your partner your true feelings.

♥

Surprising the one you love is a great way to initiate, maintain, and/or intensify any relationship. Surprises and gifts can make your mate feel loved and break up the monotony of your day-to-day routine. Just be sure to put some thought into any gift you give so that your mate can truly feel special and not puzzled by your actions.

chapter five:
don't worry, be happy

Have you ever noticed how some people seem to have a zest for life while others think that nothing ever goes their way? Who do you think most people would rather hang out with? Who would most people rather date? What about marriage? Optimism researchers have some clear answers for you.

In general, people who are more optimistic (i.e. individuals who tend to expect favorable outcomes in their lives) experience a wide variety of health, social, and emotional benefits because of their positive outlooks on life.[30] From being less stressed to experiencing less depressive episodes to being more liked by others, optimists seem to have it all together. In 1997, Dr. Amy Dicke (now Dr. Amy Dicke Bohmann), Ph.D., discovered that optimists are even preferred as romantic partners over pessimists by most individuals, regardless of their own level of optimism or pessimism.[31] The bottom line: everyone likes an optimist!

Regardless of your own views on optimism, research strongly supports the notion that being positive is an excellent and effective way to start, maintain, and intensify any relationship- romantic or platonic. For example, when meeting someone new, presenting a positive self-image is a great way to generate liking.[32] Being enthusiastic, cheerful, and energetic about life can easily make others like you. And, once you actually begin a relationship with someone, positivity continues to be extremely important for maintaining that relationship. In fact, researchers like Dr. Vicki Helgeson, Ph.D., of Carnegie Mellon University, Dr. Sandra Murray, Ph.D., of State University of New York at Buffalo, and Dr. John G. Holmes, Ph.D., of University of Waterloo, have discovered that being optimistic about your relationship predicts your satisfaction with that relationship and it actually can reduce the possibility that your relationship will end. [33] And it's not just optimists who feel this way. People who are in relationships with optimists also have greater feelings of relationship satisfaction, no matter their own level of optimism.[34]

One way to experience these relationship benefits is to incorporate positive interactions into your relationship routine. As explained by Dr. Steve McCornack, Ph.D., a professor at Michigan State University and author of *Reflect and Relate* (a popular interpersonal communication textbook), "THE most important tactic or practice for maintaining ongoing romantic involvements- and one that is more commonly overlooked- is POSITIVITY. One simply cannot overstate the significance of approaching interactions with partners with a positive frame of mind and doing what you can to lift a partner's spirits on a daily basis. Similarly, the damage wrought by complaining, insulting, sulking, and other forms of "negativity" is profound and poisonous."

Dr. McCornack is exactly right. Not only is positivity absolutely vital to feelings of happiness and closeness in your relationship, but there is also a large body of research showing that negative people usually get a bad rap.[35] For instance, researchers have discovered that pessimistic people tend to be socially rejected because many people believe that pessimists are hopeless, sad, and depressed.[36] Research has also revealed that strangers, family, and friends alike all negatively view people who are unsatisfied with themselves or their lives.[37] Furthermore, if others perceive a stigma (like pessimism) as controllable, individuals holding that stigma are perceived even more negatively than if the stigma they possess is perceived as uncontrollable.[38]

You can begin this quest for a brighter, more hopeful life with your soul mate (and yes, it is a *quest*) by first working on becoming a more optimistic person yourself and then creating a more positive climate in your relationship. But beware; overdoing it can be just as detrimental as negativity. Okay, maybe that's an exaggeration (I do that sometimes). Let's just say that it's not such a great idea to be **excessively** positive.

BECOME A MORE POSITIVE PERSON

I am an optimist. Now before you pass any judgment, I want to make it clear that I am *not* one of those bubbly, giggly, ridiculously-happy-all-of-the-time women who you (and I) secretly want to strangle (it's okay, you can admit it; we're all friends here). I know *those people*. I am *not* one of them. I don't put on a happy face for show and I sure as hell don't think that things are going well when they clearly are not. But, in the grand scheme of things, I tend to believe that positive things will happen to me. And, if I encounter heartache, sadness, depression, anger, or other negative experiences, I usually have this feeling that things *will* get better. They always do; even if only for a brief period.

If you know me, you've heard me say things like, "It always seems to work out," or "It always gets done." And I'm usually right. Things *do* seem to work out for me (I have a pretty awesome life--great husband, boy/girl twins, and a job I totally love) and I *do* always get things done (maybe not in the most timely manner--my dissertation took a little longer than planned--but I still get things done). Throughout my life, people have asked me how I have become so optimistic. It doesn't take long for me to respond with, "My Dad; definitely my Dad."

Don't worry, be happy is actually a mantra that my Dad lived by. He would try to look at the bright side of things even though it was extremely difficult for him at times. He didn't care about material things--even his much-loved cars were expendable. One time, my sister pulled his fully restored 1969 Firebird out of the driveway and dragged our metal fence along the side of the car. He didn't care. Another time, I wrecked his favorite truck into Hus' parked car (no, I was not intoxicated; it was a complete accident). He didn't care. Instead, he would ask us if *we* were okay and then he'd just fix it--or he wouldn't. You see, to him, those things didn't matter. Keeping up with the Joneses was not a concern of his. He was who he was. All of the time. He knew what was truly important in life and "things" were never on that list. He was humble. He gave people second chances (and third chances and fourth chances). And, he believed that people were inherently good.

Unbeknownst to many of his friends, my dad had a really rough life. He experienced the loss of both of his parents and older brother by the time he was 15, bouts of homelessness and being passed around from family member to family member as an adolescent, working long hours as a teenager only to be robbed by people who were supposed to take care of him, the death of his beloved sister and best friend as a young adult, the feelings of entrapment that come along with addiction, and a debilitating terminal illness for the last 12 years of his life, among other things. Needless to say, he wasn't dealt the best hand. But, he kept smiling. He kept finding joy in the small things. He would say that there was always someone else who had it worse off than him and that he was thankful for everything that he *did* have. With all of the hardship he faced, he was the epitome of an optimistic person. Again, he wasn't unrealistic about things, and believe me, he bitched about a lot of shit in his life, but overall, he could usually see the light at the end of the tunnel. And to him, it was bright.

While I inherited my upbeat ways from my dad, don't worry if you feel like you're lacking a hopeful parental figure to imitate. You can still become more optimistic. But, you have to want it. It's very difficult to change something about yourself that is so inherent to who you are as a person. You have to systematically begin to look at other people, yourself, your goals, your experiences, and your life in a positive light.

As the late Dr. Randy Pausch, Ph.D., author of *The Last Lecture*, past professor at Carnegie Mellon, and advocate of pancreatic cancer research, eloquently stated, "Experience is what you get when you didn't get what you wanted." Optimists are able to see the value (even if that value is very small) in negative experiences while pessimists tend to put another notch on the bedpost that is their terrible life with each defeatist encounter. Try to let the bad days teach you something. Try to look at important people in your life as good-intentioned (because they usually are). Try to anticipate problems that may occur in your life and- here's the kicker- formulate strategies for dealing with those problems if and when they actually happen. Optimists don't just glide through life thinking that everything will always go their way. But they also don't let the potential of negative experiences consume their everyday thoughts. Instead, they develop plans for dealing with difficult situations and when those situations present themselves, they're ready. They are then able to execute their plans and get through whatever hard time they're facing. It also helps that optimists fundamentally believe that their confrontation with negativity will be over. Still need help being more optimistic? Follow some (or all) of these tips below and you could be on your way to enjoying the benefits that optimists experience everyday.

8 Tips for Becoming
More Optimistic

Let go of things you cannot control or change.
You can only change yourself.
You cannot change other people.

Get inspired by other positive people.
Find them and become their friends.

Simplify your busy life. If you're doing things
that you hate, stop doing them. If you
hate your job, quit your bitching
and look for a new one.

Let go of the assumption that
the world is against you.

Appreciate what you have instead
of agonizing over what you don't have.

Try to eliminate words like "always"
& "never" from your vocabulary when
talking about your life. "I never get to do
anything fun" & "I'm always so unlucky"
are very pessimistic statements that
are more than likely untrue.

Keep a one-sentence happiness journal.
Every day, write down one sentence
about *something* that made you happy.

Avoid other negative people. If negative
people surround you, try not to let
their negativity get you down.

ADD MORE POSITIVITY INTO YOUR RELATIONSHIP

Dr. Phil McGraw, Ph.D., has been known to say, "It takes 1000 atta-boys to erase one negative comment." I'm sure you've heard this said before about raising children, but the same logic is extremely useful in romantic relationships as well. Dr. John Gottman, Ph.D., the Director of *The Relationship Research Institute* and Professor Emertis at the University of Washington, has shown in decades of research that happy, healthy couples tend to experience a 20 to 1 ratio in favor of positive interactions. Conflicted couples have an average 5 (positive interactions) to 1 (negative interactions) ratio and soon-to-be-divorced couples have an average .8 to 1 ratio. Thus, Dr. Gottman believes that successful, happy relationships (and especially marriages) require **at least** a 5 to 1 ratio between positive and negative interactions, respectively. I couldn't agree more.

"When Joe does something that makes me angry, it's difficult for me to remember the good stuff—the reasons why I love him. I just get consumed by all of the bad stuff that he's done in the past. It's hard for me to let go of some of that stuff; even if it's trivial."

–Liana, in a relationship with Joe since June 1987 & married since May 1989

Just think about it. Relationships are shaped by the experiences that we share with our partners. And unfortunately, we tend to let negative experiences influence our feelings about our relationships much more so than positive experiences. Think about 3 things that your partner has done to infuriate you. Well, that was easy. Now, think about 3 things that your partner has done that filled you with feelings of immense joy. Not so easy.

Still not convinced? Try on this next example for size. Imagine that your partner cheated on you. Infidelity (a very negative experience) can drastically change the dynamics of your relationship (i.e. the amount of communication, sex, physical touch, feelings of intimacy, etc.). Next, imagine that your partner took you on a surprise romantic weekend getaway to the Bahamas (I know, I wish I could do that, too!). I would argue that this could be seen as a positive experience of equal magnitude. But, the dynamics of your relationship are not likely to change in an equally positive manner.

Sure, you may feel loved and have greater feelings of commitment after this vacation, but overall, you won't experience as many immediate effects from your mate's romantic gesture as you would from something like infidelity.

The notion that a single negative experience can have a greater impact on our lives than a single positive event has been referred to by researchers as the *negativity bias*.[39] In fact, researchers have argued that "[h]umans are biased toward behaving in a manner that will avoid negative experiences, and are much more likely to recall and be influenced by negative experiences from the past."[40]

Because of this, integrating more positivity into your relationship is very important. But for many of us, this can feel like a chore. I get it, you have so many other things to worry about and finding ways to be more positive is just one more item to go on your seemingly never-ending to-do list. Or, you might also feel like you can't find things to be positive about. I promise though, once you make positivity with your partner a habit, it will not seem like a job anymore and it will be easy to find positivity in your everyday experiences. It will become part of your natural interaction patterns with one another.

Hus has not always had the most optimistic perspective on life. Okay, maybe that's a bit of an understatement. He's actually pretty darn pessimistic when it comes to a lot of things. He tends to think that something bad is destined to happen to him; especially if his life is going well (weird, right?).‡ And he sometimes lets these fears of negative future experiences swallow him whole. It's also more difficult for him to look at the bright side of a bad situation and when it comes to figuring out the intentions of others, forget about it. Hus will usually think that you are trying to screw him over in one way or another.

When his pessimism started to interfere with the quality of our relationship, we talked about it. We talked about how his negativity made me feel and about how it made Hus feel. Surprisingly, Hus didn't like thinking about all of that negative stuff as much as I didn't like hearing about it. We talked about bringing more positivity into our relationship. And we talked about how we thought we could go about doing that.

To facilitate our conversation, Hus and I talked about the things that were really important to us: happy kids, a great long-lasting marriage, a roof over our heads, enough money to pay the bills and have a little fun, a nice car (that was Hus' idea), and family and friends who support us. We then weighted those things.

---

‡ I think Hus does this because he feels like something bad *has* to happen (because it always does) and since things are going so well, the bad event must be happening soon. Go figure.

"I really want the kids to be happy and us to be happy," I said.

"Yeah, those are definitely at the top. It's also important to have supportive family and friends and some money so that we can live," he responded.

"I agree. The kids and our marriage are first. Then family, friends, and money. The rest just goes at the bottom of the list."

"Uh-huh," Hus said.

We looked at our list. We talked about everything that was good in each of the categories and everything that we didn't like, that we wished we could change, or that just sucked. It turns out that we actually had a pretty good life. Overall, our kids were great (happy, healthy, and hilarious), our relationship was strong (11 years with no deal-breaking problems), we paid our bills every month and we weren't in any severe debt (besides our mortgage), we had great family and friends, and we lived in a little house that we loved. I think it took writing it all out for Hus to see that we didn't (and he didn't) have such a bad life after all.

From that point on, Hus has made a significant, conscious effort to be more positive; at least when he's talking about our relationship and life together. Hus still has some of those feelings of fated doom, but he has worked very hard to first, think rationally about why he has those feelings and, second, recognize the small positive events in his daily life and talk about them. Below are a few activities that you and your partner can do to add more positivity into your relationship.

4 Positivity Activities

Become list-makers. Think about why you love your partner. Write this list down. And, don't just *make* the list. *Share it* with your partner. *Remember it* throughout the year as you go through the ebbs and flows of your relationship. And, *add to it* whenever your mate does something that reaffirms your love or makes you love him/her even more. Then *share it* again. Pick one or two special days each year to officially share your lists. For example, Hus and I started sharing our lists on our wedding anniversary. You could share your lists on Thanksgiving, one another's birthdays, New Year's Eve, or any other holiday throughout the year.

Focus. Spend some time concentrating on the positive things in the present and in your future together; not on the mistakes or negative events from your past. The past is the past. You can acknowledge that these things occurred, but focus the majority of your time and energy on your current life and future as a couple.

Laugh together. Laugh about the things that would usually irritate you and laugh about those silly things that the two of you encounter from time to time. You could even watch a funny movie or go on a fun date (like ice skating, bowling, or to a comedy show) to induce laughter. As you will read about later, laughter not only has a significant impact on your physical and mental well-being as an individual, but it can also increase the amount of positive interactions that the two of you share.

Apologize and forgive. Talk about things that have bothered, saddened, annoyed, or angered you (you know, those things that you just can't seem to let go of) and talk it out- with each other of course. Recognize your mate's feelings and sincerely ask for forgiveness. When your partner expresses his or her own regrets, actually accept your mate's apology. Once the two of you have discussed your past issues, **let them go**.

Like I said, Hus and I began sharing our "Why I love you" lists on our wedding anniversary. This new tradition has proven to have a significant impact our relationship. Sharing our lists has allowed (and forced) us to express ourselves emotionally, helped remind us why we're together in the first place, and it just feels good to hear wonderful things about myself when he reads me his list.

AVOID EXCESSIVE POSITIVITY

Okay, so being positive is better than being negative. It's better for you, your friendships, and your romantic relationships. But, we all can't live on a bed of roses every minute of everyday, right? At times, we may get irritated with our partners (like when dirty laundry is left on the floor), have blow-out disagreements (you know, the ones about your in-laws), or simply misunderstand each other ("You wanted me to do what?"). Events like these test our ability to look on the bright side. What should we do in these situations? Should we have big arguments about everything that bugs us (marking these incidents up as *yet another* negative interaction in our relationship) or should we look for the positive aspects of these not-so-positive experiences (sometimes ignoring our true feelings to avoid experiencing negativity)? How do *you* deal with the negative experiences you go through with your mate?

I can honestly say that I have fallen victim to completely ignoring them on several occasions. And I've also been known to have a major melt down about negative experiences. I'm just one of those pick-one-extreme-and-stick-to-it kinds of people. I know, I know, it's bad. I'm definitely an optimistic person, but sometimes, it seems absolutely impossible to see the light at the end of the long tunnel of aggravation. I try to pick my battles and turn a blind eye to the insignificant things that bug me (I don't want to watch my marriage spiral out of control because I couldn't handle the way that Hus leaves hair in the sink after shaving or forgets to do the laundry, right?). But I'll admit that many times I fail to discuss (i.e. try to remain positive by avoiding the problem) something that has really affected me--like my secret qualms about the unequal household duties that occurred when our twins were under the age of one (Well, I guess Hus knows now). Needless to say, this is not the best way to make use of my ability to be positive.

Researchers have identified many strategies (and given a few of them fancy names) that individuals use to keep the peace during trying times. For instance, some people focus their attention on their mates' other positive characteristics ("So what if he's late all of the time, he *is* really thoughtful."), voice their concern ("I'm a bit troubled by the dishes on the counter"), or simply remain loyal and hope for the best ("I know that she'll come around").[41] One of the more effective ways for partners to cope with such negative events is through the use of *benevolent cognitions*, that is, "interpreting negative events in ways that allow each partner to maintain positive views of the relationship and of each other."[42] Holding yourself accountable during squabbles with your partner and not condemning him or her for negative events will help you and your relationship. Researchers have found that couples who use this strategy tend to experience high levels of relationship satisfaction and stability over time.[43]

This line of research, however, has only focused on minor, more everyday negative experiences, as opposed to serious relationship problems. A 2008 study[44] by Dr. James McNulty, Ph.D., and Dr. Erin O'Mara, Ph.D., of University of Tennessee, and Dr. Benjamin Karney,

Ph.D., of UCLA examined whether the strategy of *benevolent cognitions* is also effective with couples facing intense marital problems. To examine this issue, the researchers followed 251 newly married couples over a four-year period. They discovered that the impact of *benevolent cognitions* on relationship satisfaction and stability depends on the amount of *initial* negativity in the relationship. People who make positive attributions of negative experiences are only more likely to have higher marital satisfaction in their relationships *if* they are already involved in marriages with minimal to moderate marital problems. And, couples with serious marital problems who use the *benevolent cognition* strategy tend to experience decreases in overall marital satisfaction and stability over time.

Coping with negativity in your relationship by focusing on the positive aspects of the situation and not blaming one another for what has happened is a great strategy to maintain or improve marital satisfaction for couples that have mild to moderate marital problems. However, this strategy is not very effective at maintaining or improving marital satisfaction for couples that have serious marital problems because it lowers their motivation to address problems directly.

Okay, so positivity is good, to an extent. It's really important that you talk to your mate about serious issues in your relationship. But, when the tiffs are inconsequential, which many of them are, try not to sweat the small stuff and remain positive.

♥

Overall, continuing to be optimistic and upbeat will prove to be one of the best things you can do for you and your relationship.

chapter six: LAUGH

H umor has been shown to be a significant predictor of satisfaction in relationships by several studies over the last few decades.[45] Incorporating a little humor into your daily routine can be a wonderful addition to the life you share with your partner. Playful teasing, inside jokes, giving gag gifts, and reminiscing about funny events from the past with your partner have all been shown to help keep established relationships going strong and even help repair relationships that are heading south.

HUMOROUS RELATIONSHIPS

To begin my explanation of the importance of laughter in relationships, I'd like to tell a story my parents. As a child, I always knew that my mom and dad were soul mates. From the way my mom would watch her animated husband tell a story, to my dad's desire to always tell his wife that he loved her, to the way that they bickered in the car about who *really* made them late, I always knew that they were meant to be together. So, what was their secret? They were best friends who took time to laugh. That's it.

> "Being able to laugh at each other is really important. I'm not friends with non-funny people, and I cannot even imagine being in a relationship with someone who doesn't get my sense of humor or who can't make me laugh at all the ridiculous things life throws my way."
>
> *-Molly, in a relationship with Red since 2007*

That was their secret (well, let's be serious, they each had many relationship skills that they developed and utilized for over 30 years, but this skill was particularly prevalent to me). Whether my parents were arguing about their budget, sharing their deepest feelings and thoughts, or just talking about their day, they were always talking, and more importantly, always laughing. Laughing was very important in our house.

My dad, a hilarious story-teller who laughed at his own jokes, and my mom, an amazing listener who has been known to laugh until she cries, spent hours actually enjoying each other's company. They could laugh about anything. While my dad was the main joke-teller, my mom would tease my dad about all of his little quirks, which also tended to be quite amusing. They laughed when they were celebrating, they laughed at the end of an argument, and they even laughed when my dad became terminally ill. Once my father knew that his life was going to end, he and my mom decided to write his eulogy, together. Even during his final days on earth, my dad managed to make his eulogy really funny. To additionally honor him, and all that he stood for, my mom invited friends and family to share funny stories they had about my dad at his memorial service in 2006. So, even in his passing, my mom was laughing. Laughing got them through many tough times in their lives. It helped them grow closer as a couple, it gave them an excuse to be silly, and it showed them what was truly important in life.

A large body of research has supported the idea that my parents' ability to share laughter and other positive emotions together significantly enhanced their marriage for over 30 years. For instance, Dr. John Gottman, Ph.D., a psychologist, researcher, and author of *Why Marriages Succeed or Fail* and several other successful marriage books, and his colleagues have conducted numerous studies examining relationship stability among married couples. One of these studies[46] specifically discovered that incorporating positive emotions (including humor and affection) into marital interactions was the *only* significant predictor of both satisfaction and stability during the first six years of marriage. Similarly, another one of Gottman's studies[47] identified humor as a significant characteristic of happily married, stable, middle-aged and elderly couples. Furthermore, other researchers[48] have examined marriages lasting at least 45 years and discovered that laughing together was cited as one of the top three reasons for marital success, with many of the individuals in these marriages stating that they would go out of their way to engage in humorous interactions with their partners.

HUMOROUS RECOLLECTIONS

As previously mentioned, it's not just important to laugh with your partner about humorous events *as they are happening*. Reminiscing about the funny times from your past can also have a positive impact on your relationship. In a 2007 study,[49] psychologists from Appalachian State University assessed the relationship satisfaction of 52 couples before and after they engaged in a joint interview with a researcher. During the interview, each couple was asked to reminisce about two events from their past, with each partner talking about one event. While there were four different kinds of experiences examined in the study (events where you shared laughter with your partner, events where you laughed with a family member or friend, events where you shared a positive experience with your partner, or events where you shared a positive experience with a family member or friend), each couple was only asked to describe one of the four event types.

This study revealed that couples who reminisced about shared

> "We try not to take ourselves too seriously, so we do a lot of light-hearted joking around about various things. For example, most recently every time a kiss lingers a little longer than usual, I'm bound to open my eyes to see Jon staring wide-eyed at me an inch away from my face, which may not seem romantic (it's kind of creepy really), but it keeps us laughing, and fun love is the best love."
>
> *-Kindra, in a relationship with Jon since January 2004 & married since September 2008*

laughter from their past experienced increased feelings of relationship satisfaction directly following the discussion of that event (when compared to couples who described one of the other three event types-laughter with someone else, positive event together, and positive event with someone else). This finding shows that talking with your partner about past shared experiences where you both laughed about something is more important than reflecting on experiences that were merely positive without any laughter.

Hus and I are constantly talking about all of the hilarity that we've experienced in our life together. For instance, whenever we pass a construction site, we talk about that one time when we were with my best friend and her boyfriend "exploring" an abandoned construction site in the middle of the night (ah, the days when I could stay up all night long and still function the next day... well kind of function) when all of the sudden—I fell into a 8-foot deep hole in the ground. And got the wind knocked out of me. So I couldn't yell. But, I could hear everyone yelling for me, "Jennie! Where are you? Are you hiding? This isn't funny!" They finally figured out where I was and pulled me out. Hilarious.

Well... it's funny to us.

And then there was this other time when Hus was trying to open a window and it kept falling down. Up, down, up, down, up, down. So, he brilliantly decided to put a bottle of hairspray in the window to prop it up. This caused a significant amount of sticky, smelly hairspray to be misted all over his face and directly into his eyes. I couldn't contain myself. He later claimed that he thought the bottle was empty and that nothing was going to spray out, but we both know that he just wasn't thinking clearly. We laughed together as I helped him get the sticky substance out of his ears.

Okay, well maybe these stories aren't very funny on paper. But they're funny to us, and that's what matters, right? The point is to not just laugh about funny things as they're happening, but to also make an effort to reminisce about these hilarious occurrences later to further enhance your relationship satisfaction.

HUMOROUS CONFLICT

In addition to enhancing relationship satisfaction and stability, laughter can easily break any tension that you and your partner may be experiencing. In fact, research has shown that jokes, which facilitate your relationship or reduce tension, are extremely effective in conflict situations.[50] Instead of taking everything so seriously all of the time, laughing about life's mishaps with your partner has the potential to bring you closer together and even help you solve the problem you're facing.

Have you ever been in the heat of an argument, when your partner suddenly cracked a joke? How did you feel? Did it help or hinder the resolution of your conflict? For me, my reaction to this seemingly contradictory event would depend on a few things: (1) the level of anger I possessed at the time, (2) the strength of my desire to be angry, (3) the severity of the argument, and of course, (4) the hilarity of the joke.

In our marriage, we both have been known to insert wisecracks into our daily conversations, whether it is about conflict or something else. And, I'm certain that Hus and I both have felt enjoyment and have also been extremely frustrated by one of our humorous comments during a disagreement. For instance, when our twins were only a few weeks old, Hus and I were sleep deprived and needless to say, a little stressed out. We had been arguing about not having enough time to clean the house and we took it upon ourselves to call out each other's lack of cleanliness, "You haven't done the dishes for weeks!" "Well, you haven't taken out the garbage in months!" We knew what needed to happen to resolve this conflict, but at the time, we decided to criticize one another instead. During our disagreement, I was pouring my recently pumped breast milk into a container to put in the fridge. I married two containers of milk into one, and for some reason, I then decided to shake it… without screwing on the lid. Milk went *everywhere*. An hour of my life was now on the kitchen floor. We both looked at one another and started uncontrollably laughing. We got on our hands and knees, together, cleaned up the milk and apologized about the accusations that were made only a few minutes earlier. Hus and I then divvied up the household chores and agreed that we would both keep up with our respective jobs. In this situation, laughter was the referee that we so desperately needed. It broke up our fight and gave us a minute to re-evaluate our game plan.

Research by Drs. Lorne Campbell, Ph.D., Rod Martin, Ph.D., and Jennie R. Ward, Ph.D., Psychologists at the University of Western Ontario, investigated how different types of humor used during arguments influence relationship satisfaction and conflict resolution.[51] They looked at four styles of humor, two of which are considered healthy (*affiliative* and *self-enhancing*) and two that are considered unhealthy (*aggressive* and *self-defeating*).[52] According to Dr. Campbell and his colleagues, "*Affiliative* humor involves saying funny things, telling jokes, and engaging in spontaneous witty banter in order to amuse others, to facilitate relationships, and to reduce interpersonal tensions in a way that is affirming of both oneself and others."[53] Individuals who use *affiliative* humor are able to make other people laugh, while still maintaining a respectful attitude towards oneself and others, and tend to be known as "jokesters" by their friends and family. *Self-enhancing* humor refers to using humor to adjust or change an individual's feelings. People use this type of humor to cope with stress. Individuals will make these jokes or comments during hard times and also during everyday life events. Individuals use *aggressive* humor to demean or manipulate others. *Aggressive* humor includes insulting, criticism, sarcasm, teasing, or other forms of derogatory humor. *Aggressive* humor is used to enhance oneself at the expense of others. *Self-defeating* humor involves doing or saying demeaning things about oneself to amuse others. People who use *self-defeating* humor often degrade themselves for a laugh and then laugh along with others at their own expense. Since most previous research has shown that *self-enhancing* and *self-defeating* humor has little to no effect on perceptions of relationship satisfaction and also based on the fact that researchers who rated participants in the current study were not able to identify many instances of the two humor styles, Drs. Campbell, Martin, and Ward decided to only focus their study on *affiliative* and *aggressive* styles of humor.

After 98 couples participated in a three-phase study, the researchers came to several conclusions about the use of humor during conflict:

- Men used *affiliative* humor more often than women.

- Men and women both used *aggressive* humor to the same extent.

- People were more satisfied with their relationships when their partners used more *affiliative* (as opposed to more *aggressive*) humor during conflicts.

- People felt a lot closer to their partners after a disagreement when their partners and when they themselves used more *affiliative* (as opposed to more *aggressive*) humor during an argument.

- When partners used more *affiliative* humor during the discussion of conflict, their distress was lowered. And oppositely—an individual's own use of *affiliative* humor had no effect on their own distress.

- When individuals used *aggressive* humor with their partners during conflict, their distress increased, but when partners used *aggressive* humor during the discussion of conflict, there was minimal impact on their own distress.

- People who had partners who used more *affiliative* humor during conflict reported that they were more able to resolve their differences, where individuals who used more *aggressive* humor reported little to no resolution of their conflict.

To summarize, couples who use *affiliative* humor during conflict also tend to be happier, be more satisfied with their relationships, experience higher levels of intimacy, and are better able to find a solution to their conflict than couples who use *aggressive* humor during an disagreement. Based on this research, it seems as though *affiliative* humor is a great way for you and your mate to experience a wide variety of benefits during and after a conflict interaction.

Although I definitely believe in the power of humor and laughter in close relationships, I'm still not completely sold on using it during *every* argument. It would depend on many things for me. For instance, I think humor would be great in an argument about your partner's driving abilities, but it would likely further infuriate me in an argument about infidelity. I guess the real tip here is that if you want to use humor during a pesky quarrel, you should try jokes that facilitate your relationship or reduce tension and stay away from negative teasing, insults, and sarcasm. Who knows, maybe humorous conflict is the way to go.

If, and when, you decide to integrate some humor into your daily conversations (about conflict or anything for that matter), here are a few tips so that you can be as funny as you want to be.

> "Over the years, Steve and I have learned to laugh at each other and at life. Keeping the humor in our relationship makes everything more interesting. We're constantly laughing and it keeps our relationship new and exciting. The more we laugh, the closer we get."
>
> -Samantha, in a relationship with Steve since December 2001 & married since August 2007

5 Tips for Being Funny

Exaggerate

A little dramatization of the truth never hurt anyone, right? Well, as long as there are good intentions behind the exaggeration, it's obvious that you're exaggerating, and of course... it's funny! In my experience, exaggerations are even funnier when they are specific instead of general. So, instead of telling your partner that you watched *The Wizard of Oz* a lot as a kid, you could say, "I must have watched *The Wizard of Oz* 587,924 times as a kid!" I'm definitely a fan of exaggeration.

Use Puns

A pun is a clever play on words that either mixes up words that sound similar (ex: genes and jeans) or words that are spelled the same with different meanings (ex: an ear of corn and the ears on your head). The best puns are silly, delivered quickly, and spontaneous. For example, if your partner is putting aluminum foil on a bowl of leftovers, you could say, "Ah, foiled again!" Here, "foiled" can refer to the actual aluminum foil your mate is using or it can refer to the fact that the leftover food has not been eaten yet again (foiled can also mean "stopped" or "thwarted"). Even though puns are usually viewed as a bit cheesy, they can still result in laughter.

Pay Attention and Listen

Funny situations are everywhere. Pay attention to what's going on and make a comment about something you find to be funny, even if it's only mildly funny.

Don't Offend Anyone

Probably the most important tip here is to not cross the line when using humor. You don't want to offend your partner. Negative teasing, insults, and name-calling are not effective ways to use humor. Know the boundaries and stay on your side.

Use Unique Language

Putting words together that most people would not usually combine in their everyday speech is funny. For instance, you could say, "I highly enjoy that" or "That is an example of sensational perfection" instead of just telling someone that you like something. Or, you could comment on something minor in a more serious way. Telling your mate "That is a truly unfortunate catastrophe" when he or she has spilled a shot of vodka will likely get a laugh out of him or her.

As I reflect upon my own marriage, I realize that my parents' use of laughter definitely rubbed off on me. Hus and I love cracking jokes with one another on a daily basis. And, when I think about it, I think it does help strengthen our bond. Looking at my parents' relationship, I've learned that life is too short for it to be serious all of the time, that you can never tell someone that you love them too much, and that you should always take time out of everyday to laugh with the people you love. Thanks, Mom and Dad.

chapter seven:

make love, not scrapbooks

P ut down the scissors, glitter paper, and double-sided tape. Step away from your super-deluxe scrapbooking station with your 42 built-in paper trays (one for every color type and pattern genre), ribbon rack that holds 37 of your favorite colorful strips of fabric, and 29 jars filled with buttons, fasteners, and other embellishments. Walk out of your craft room and get back into the bedroom.

Whether you're an avid scrapbooker, miniature train set aficionado, wine connoisseur, or car show enthusiast, many of us have hobbies (or other activities, obligations, and responsibilities) that consume our lives. Although these interests may be fun and exciting, many times, the sexual relationship that we have with our partners is not given top priority.

Let me get this discussion going by posing a few questions. First, how many times a week do you have sex? Okay, maybe we need to back it up a bit: How many times a *month* do you have sex? If you can't answer that one, you *definitely* need to read this. How about this question: Do you *enjoy* the sex that you have? Are you sexually satisfied in your relationship? Here's an even better one: how often do you orgasm?

What if I told you that having sex, actually enjoying it, and especially orgasming multiple times a week is related to numerous health benefits, emotional well-being, and even a longer life! Would you put down this book and head off to the bedroom?

Well, in the last 30 years, researchers have discovered that engaging in sexual activities multiple times a week is related to numerous physical, psychological, and relationship benefits including, but not limited to, a lower risk of heart disease,[54] longer life span,[55] lower levels of depression,[56] increased self-esteem,[57] and enhanced feelings of affection, intimacy, and closeness with a sexual partner.[58] See the table below for an extended list of benefits.

Benefits of Having Sex, Enjoying It, and Orgasming

Physical Benefits
Reduction in the risk for and incidence of heart disease
Decreased risk of prostate cancer
Lower risk for and incidence of breast cancer
Lower incidence of endometriosis
Heightened ability to sleep
Longer life

Psychological Benefits
Decreased need for psychiatric medications
Lower levels of depression
Reduced feelings of stress
Increased self-esteem
Better quality of life

Relationship Benefits
Increased feelings of intimacy and closeness
Higher levels of relationship satisfaction
Longer relationships

This list was created from an article by Whipple, Knowles, & Davis (2007)

Unfortunately, many couples are plagued with dissatisfying sex lives,[59] with some marriages even becoming sexless (i.e. couples who engage in sex less than 10 times per year) overtime. You may be in one of these relationships and that's okay. Hopefully by the end of this chapter, you will better understand the importance of rekindling the fire in your bedroom *and* better understand how you can go about doing that.

Correlation Explanation

When individuals do this type of research, they cannot determine which variable is the cause and which is the effect. They can only say that there is a relationship or association between the two variables. For example, if you hear that people who shop are also happy, you know that there is a relationship between shopping and happiness. However, you don't know whether shopping causes people to be happy or whether happiness causes people to shop; both seem valid. For correlational research to be more rigorous, researchers must control for any other variables that might impact the strength of the relationship between the two variables under question. Back to the example, you might say that people who shop are happy because most people who shop are also wealthy, which could additionally contribute to happiness. A good researcher would control for this variable (i.e. wealth) by asking participants to report their income and seeing if the majority of shoppers were also wealthy. If wealth doesn't matter, then the relationship between happiness and shopping is considered stronger. The problem is that we just don't know which came first: the shopping or the happiness. This does **not** mean that correlational studies are worthless. Quite the contrary. Significant relationships found between two variables can provide us with very important knowledge. You just need to use your critical thinking skills when reading about this type of research.

As I've already stated, the benefits associated with having lots of sex seem to be endless. But, what if you don't like the sex that you're having? Sexual satisfaction plays a huge role in whether or not you experience these advantages. In fact, a large body of research has shown that *liking* your sex life is extremely important to your relationship. Specifically, individuals' satisfaction with their sex lives has been shown to be positively associated with their overall relationship satisfaction (as sexual satisfaction increases, so does relationship satisfaction) among both heterosexual[60] and homosexual[61] couples. It's important to note here that these studies have been correlational in nature and therefore do not show which variable causes the other. So, it is unclear as to whether being sexually satisfied causes people to have high relationship satisfaction or if being satisfied with your relationship causes you to be sexually satisfied. Despite not knowing the directionality of this relationship, the association between sexual satisfaction and relationship satisfaction is strong and should definitely be taken into consideration when trying to determine the cause of dissatisfaction in either of these areas.

Several researchers[62] have also studied the link between sexual satisfaction and relationship stability overtime. For example, using data from the *Early Years of Marriage Project*, Drs. Jean Oggins, Ph.D., of the University of Professional Studies, Douglass Leber, Ph.D., of the University of Denver, and Joeseph Veroff, Ph.D., of the University of Michigan examined sexual satisfaction during the first year and fourth year of marriage. The researchers[63] discovered that couples who were less sexually satisfied during their first year of marriage were more likely to be divorced by their fourth year than individuals who were more sexually satisfied in their first year. In addition, Drs. John N. Edwards, Ph.D., of Virginia Tech and Alan Booth, Ph.D., of Penn State University [64] found that married individuals who reported having more sexual problems during an initial interview were more likely to be divorced three years later than individuals who reported less sexual problems. So, if you don't like sex in the beginning of your marriage and you get divorced a few years down the road, your or your partner's sexual dissatisfaction may have contributed to your marriage's demise. Furthermore, researchers[65] have asked individuals who recently ended a relationship to either evaluate a list of reasons or to disclose their own reasoning for the break-up. In this line of research, sexual problems and/or sexual incompatibility are often rated as at least moderately important.

To summarize, having sex and being sexually satisfied are very important when it comes to our physical health, mental well-being, and significant relationships. So why do some people still have less-than-stellar sex lives? Although most people know that sex is important, they don't know where to make improvements. When I ask couples why they think they don't have enough sex, there are three typical responses. First, "I don't like the sex that we do have, so why would I want to do it more often?" Second, "I just can't get into the mood." And lastly, "We don't have enough time to have sex." If you fall into one of these three categories, good. Let me clarify: I don't say "good" because I'm glad that you are experiencing one of these issues. Instead, I believe that it is good because I have some useful information for you that can hopefully help you want to have more sex and experience the aforementioned benefits.

"I DON'T LIKE THE SEX WE'RE HAVING."

One of the best ways to improve your sex life is to open the lines of communication between you and your partner. Studies have revealed that disclosing your sexual likes and dislikes to your mate can improve your sexual and relationship satisfaction, bring you closer as a couple, increase feelings of intimacy and trust between the two of you, and even increase pleasure during sexual activities.[66] Openly talking about sexual desires, however, is a difficult conversation to have for most Americans.[67] Telling your partner what you like and dislike in the bedroom by giving sexual feedback can be overwhelming. These feelings of apprehension are expected and completely acceptable. Instead of taking you through an entire communication skill-training program, I decided to provide some basic guidelines to follow if, and when, you decide to express your sexual likes and dislikes to your partner.[68]

4 Sexual Feedback Guidelines

Maintain a Positive Tone
Why? Keeping up a positive mood can not only help open the lines of communication about this sensitive topic, but it can also enhance your partner's confidence and improve his or her motivation to continue practicing pleasurable behaviors or change behaviors that may be less pleasurable.

How? Compliment your partner about his or her sexual skills, sandwich a dislike between two likes, and utilize positive, affirming language that encourages your partner.

Give Clear, Detailed Descriptions
Why? Using clear, descriptive words when discussing sexual issues can help to improve your sexual feedback skill, which in turn, can enhance your sexual experience. Clear and specific details help your partner fully understand exactly what you want from him or her.

How? Describe specific behaviors or techniques with descriptive and vivid words. For example, you could say "left side of my vagina" instead of "over there."

Be Sensitive

Why? "It is very important to remember that a flat-out critique of [a] partner's sexual abilities not only creates conflict in [the] relationship, but it is also mean!"[x] Also, insensitive messages may threaten your partner's self-confidence and feelings of self-efficacy.

How? To be sensitive, you should show appreciation for past sexual behaviors whether they were pleasurable or not, state the value you have for your partner's efforts to enhance sexual pleasure in your relationship, express empathy and concern, and communicate confidence in your partner's ability to improve his or her sexual performance abilities. Also, you should offer suggestions instead of giving orders, acknowledge that some feedback could and should be rejected by your partner because it may not be something that he or she wants or likes to do, directly express the optional nature of complying with your disclosure, seek permission to offer sexual feedback in the first place, explicitly recognize your partner's feelings about, and perceptions of, the desired sexual behaviors or techniques being expressed, and focus on the importance of enhancing the sexual pleasure of both you and your partner.

Be Realistic

Why? Being realistic about the amount and kind of feedback an individual can receive during any one interaction will help to not overwhelm your mate.

How? Limit your feedback to 1-3 issues during each interaction and comment only on areas in which your partner is fully capable of improving.

*Guidelines adapted from Gill Rosier (2011)

Let's say that you already feel confident in your ability to talk about your sexual desires with your partner and you're still sexually dissatisfied. Another suggestion is for you and your partner to try new sexual positions and techniques. There are a wide variety of resources available to you to help with this. First, the Internet has a wealth of information on this topic. For instance, Cosmopolitan Magazine's website has a column they call the "Sex Position of the Week" that could be helpful. Also, you could browse the sexual position texts (like a Kamasutra book) in the sexual health aisle of your local bookstore or library. You could get a book, try a different sexual position at each sexual encounter and discuss the proverbial ups and downs of each afterwards. Trying something new may be able to increase your sexual satisfaction.

"I JUST CAN'T GET IN THE MOOD."

Not being able to "get into it" is an extremely common problem among many couples around the world. Depending on the root of the problem (i.e. psychological, relational, or physical), some of the suggestions on the next few pages may be valuable to you.

If nothing seems to work, you could try just kissing. Kissing is one of the more sensual acts you can do with your mate. It has the ability to enhance your sexual experience while also making you feel loved and wanted. Interestingly, researchers have long studied different forms of physical affection, and have found that kissing also reduces signs of distress.[69] "Highly affectionate adults report less stress, lower susceptibility to depression, greater overall mental health, and higher satisfaction with their romantic relationships than do their less affectionate counterparts."[70]

Dr. Wendy Hill, Ph.D., a professor of psychology at Lafayette College and kissing researcher, has explained that kissing releases chemicals in the brain that trigger a wide variety of emotions. From feelings of closeness and intimacy to feelings of happiness and euphoria, kissing can greatly benefit your relationship.

16 Ways to Boost Your Sexual Desire

Talk Dirty
Men and women can both benefit from a little risqué conversation. Many times, dirty talk can make your mate feel desired, sexy, and naughty. All of which are great sensations to experience when you're getting ready to do the nasty.

Set the Mood

Getting out the candles, turning down the lights, and playing some soft music can all set the mood for love in your house. Doing these romantic things for your partner doesn't only have the ability to intensify sexual feelings, but they can also bring you closer as a couple.

Get Enough Sleep

Lacking the proper amount of sleep can negatively impact many parts of your life, including your libido. In addition, it's really hard to get excited about sex when you're exhausted. Try getting 7+ hours of sleep every night and see if you're more interested in getting it on.

Exercise

I know it's hard to believe, but exercising can actually give you *more* energy. And, if you exercise regularly, you'll begin to feel more confident with your body and you'll likely become more willing to show it off between the sheets.

Eat Healthier

Eating three balanced meals a day will make you look and feel great. And when you feel good, you'll have more energy and more confidence, which can help you get in the mood.

Massage

Not only does massage have the ability to lower anxiety, alleviate pain, relax muscles, and increase joint mobility, but romantic, sensual massage can also increase intimacy and feelings of love between two lovers. So, make a sexy play list on your iPod and get ready rub hot oils all over your lover.

Reduce Stress

There's no denying it- most of us are stressed the hell out. Unfortunately, many of us are involved in unnecessary activities that just add to our stress levels. Try to cut out some of these nonessential responsibilities in your life. If being less stressed out isn't a turn-on, I don't know what else is.

Be Dangerous

Sometimes a little danger can spark something in your relationship. Going skydiving, rock climbing, or ride some roller coasters and use the feelings of euphoria created by dopamine and adrenaline flowing through your body to create some excitement in the bedroom.

Stop Smoking

Smoking isn't just bad for your lungs. Studies have shown that smoking can cause men to have a low sperm count and can decrease the strength of your sex drive.

Consult a Therapist

You and/or your partner may also want to talk to a therapist, psychiatrist, or counselor about your issues with sexual desire. Find a local practitioner, schedule an appointment, and work out your sexual desire difficulties with a professional.

Role-Play

Role-playing is a great way to keep things interesting in your relationship, which is sometimes a cause of low sex drive. You could role-play at home or role-play out on a date. Role-playing is adventurous and a lot of fun. And, it could easily light a flame in your relationship.

Watch Porn

Not surprisingly, watching people have sex may enhance your own desire to have sex. But, make sure that both of you are comfortable with this. Whipping out a porno before sex without your partner's knowledge could easily offend your partner and produce results that are opposite of what you hoped for. So, watching porn can definitely boost your libido, but both of you have to want to watch it.

Use Sex Toys

Many times, sex toys are able to do things that humans are just incapable of doing. This is nothing to be ashamed of. If you or your partner has trouble orgasming or if you would like your orgasms to be even more intense than they already are, sex toys are a great way to achieve your goals. And, they're not just for women anymore. There are plenty of sex toys that help men achieve more pleasure, you just need to choose the one that's best for you.

Reconnect

With all of the stress that goes along with working, managing a household, raising kids, trying to have a social life, or keeping up with hobbies, sometimes romantic relationships suffer. Reconnect with your partner by turning off your Blackberry and departing on a romantic get-a-way for the weekend, having an uninterrupted conversation about your innermost thoughts about your special bond, or going on a unique, picturesque date for just the two of you. Spending quality time together where you talk about the relationship can enhance feelings of intimacy and closeness, which are necessary for sexual desire.

Take Vitamins

Vitamins A, B, and C, iron supplements, and zinc all have the ability to increase sexual desire in different ways. While vitamins A, B, C, and zinc can enhance your fertility, iron can give you the energy needed to go all night long.

Ask your Doctor

If you feel like you have a physical problem that is causing you to have a low sexual desire, talk to your doctor. Sometimes, hormone imbalances, certain prescription drugs, anemia, diabetes, an actual sexual dysfunction, your blood pressure, specific types of cancer, particular STDs, or other physical ailments are the cause of a low libido. Get your annual physical and ask your doctor about whether some of these things could be causing your sexual desire problems.

*Some of these suggestions were adapted from the
Nerds Do It Better series on www.100BestDatingSites.com

Dr. Laura Berman, LCSW, Ph.D., a sex therapist and author of numerous sexual health books who has made regular appearances on *The Today Show* and *Oprah*, suggests that couples engage in 10 minutes of uninterrupted kissing every single day. She goes on to say that this should be *just kissing*; not kissing that leads to other sexual acts. So, in addition to your *sexual act kissing*, you should also partake in a 10-minute kiss session with your partner each and every day. Making out just to make out (with no other sexual strings attached) is great for your relationship. But don't forget about all of those little pecks through out the day. Those matter, too! Kissing your mate hello and goodbye or for no reason at all is also great for your relationship.

So, kiss your partner first thing in the morning and then again right before bed. Kiss your partner when you leave for work and when you come back home. Kiss your partner when you're just sitting on the couch and when he or she does something thoughtful or kind. Just kiss.

"WE JUST DON'T HAVE ENOUGH TIME."

I'm not sure how I can be any more clear with this one: make time! Sex is an extremely important part of our lives. Even if making time to you means once a week, you should *always* make time to share these intimate (and very beneficial) moments with your partner. And don't give me that, "but we both work and we have kids and..." nonsense. My husband and I have rambunctious 2-year-old twins and we both have full-time jobs. Believe me, we're busy.

With all of the writing (like for my blog, academic conferences, journal articles, and book-writing), teaching (I teach 4 undergraduate classes per semester at James Madison University), meeting with students (sometimes I think that this is all I do!), child-rearing (twins!), cleaning (okay, you got me--I don't do a whole lot of that), and driving (Hus and I have a on-again-off-again arrangement with sharing a car), all I really want to do at the end of the day is veg-out watching some junk television, eat a tub of Edy's Slow Churned ice cream, and go the hell to sleep--for the entire night without being woken up by one of those small people who live in the room next to ours. The pure exhaustion that I experience sometimes causes sex to be one of the last things on my mind. I know, how could this happen to me when a large amount of my research focuses on how to enhance sexual satisfaction in romantic relationship? Well, shit happens. And, I'm only human.

Fortunately, one of the things that Hus and I have learned over the last several years is that there is absolutely NO SHAME in scheduling sex with one another. It may not seem particularly sexy and it's definitely not spontaneous, but let's be serious, how many of us actually have the time to *spontaneously* have sex 3-4 times a week?

Below are the two main reasons why you and your mate should follow suite and create your own "sex calendar" of sorts.

First, many couples will try and justify the fact that they are not having enough sex. And, one of the most common reasons given is that one or both partners are too busy for sex. Life is hectic. Believe me, I get it. But I think it's important to realize that you will *always* be busy. Life is not going to magically slow down for you to have sex with your partner. And it sure as hell is not going to slow down a few times a week. The take-home message: you can't wait until you have more time because that day may never happen. You have to consciously set time aside for sex.

"We try to squeeze in as much alone time as possible, but with 2 kids, this is a challenge. Great sex and date nights are important, don't get me wrong, but they aren't practical as everyday activities when you have kids that still don't sleep through the night. So we make it a part of our everyday activities to flirt, tease, and playfully show our love for each other. The old saying "it's the little things" really rings true here. It's squeezing his butt when I pass him in the kitchen, it's kissing each other whenever we leave the house or come home, it's whispering sexy suggestions in his ear even though we know there's no time for sex right now, it's him slyly sneaking his hand up my shirt or shorts while I'm cooking and kissing my neck... it's those things that keep the spark alive."

-Amanda, in a relationship with Fernando since July 2002
and married since September 2007

Second, many people also believe that both partners have to be completely "in the mood" to have sex, and especially to have *good* sex. Unfortunately, if you decide to wait until both you and your partner are sexually aroused and ready to get it on, you might just have to wait forever. People are different. You and your partner may not be on the same sexual clock as one another. I know, you probably feel like you *used* to share the same sexual wavelength, but another interesting thing about people is that they change. You and your partner's sex drives may change over time, which could allow you to get out of sync more often than you're used to. It's important to note that this discrepancy is *not* a sign of your relationship's imminent demise. Quite the contrary. It's actually your *response* to these changes that can help predict your future together. Having sex on a regular basis, regardless of how hot-and-heavy you're feeling at that scheduled moment, is a great response to this potential problem in the bedroom. And anyways, most people tend to "get in the mood" once they start.

The fact of the matter is that spontaneous sex where both of you are truly excited, exceptionally passionate, and deeply involved is likely going to happen less often than you and your partner would like. So, although the thought of creating a sex calendar may not be an alluring concept for you, it can help guarantee that you'll be more sexually active, which as you know, can help you get one step closer to achieving those benefits to an active and satisfying sex life.

In the end, sex is important! It's a crucial component of your own psychological and physical well-being, the relationship satisfaction you experience, and your relationship's success. "Sex is more than an act of pleasure, it's the ability to be able to feel so close to a person, so connected, so comfortable that it's almost breathtaking to the point you feel you can't take it. And at this moment you're part of them."[71]

chapter eight:

heart the hell out of your mate

"I can't wait to grow old with you" is what Hus whispered in my ear at our wedding ceremony. At the time, it was exactly what I needed *and wanted* to hear. Telling your partner how you feel about your relationship and your future together is essential to maintaining and intensifying the bond that the two of you share. One of the best ways to go about doing this is to offer assurances.

BENEFITS OF ASSURANCES

Drs. Daniel Canary, Ph.D., of Arizona State University and Laura Stafford, Ph.D., of Ohio State University discovered that offering assurances is one of the more prominent strategies that individuals use to maintain, enhance, or repair their romantic relationships (with the other four main strategies being: creating a social network, being open, sharing tasks, and being positive).[72] You can pledge your dedication to your partner by demonstrating your togetherness, stressing your commitment, implying that your relationship has a future, and showing your faithfulness.[73]

Drs. Canary and Stafford discussed in one of their book chapters that studies have shown that individuals who express their commitment to their partners are more likely to experience satisfaction in their relationships than individuals who don't.[74] In addition to relationship satisfaction, assurances have also been found to be a significant predictor of commitment and liking in close relationships, with individuals in engaged and married relationships using them more often than people who are just dating.[75] Overall, offering assurances can allow your partner to feel loved, secure, and content.

HOW TO ASSURE

Whether you tell your partner directly ("I think we should move-in together") or indirectly ("You know, Jack and Jill just went on a romantic vacation, isn't that nice?"), verbally (saying "I'm gonna marry you") or nonverbally (wearing a wedding band), emphasizing your loyalty, devotion, and faithfulness is a key component to long-lasting, happy, healthy relationships. Here are 21 ways that you can demonstrate your dedication to the one you love.

21 Ways to Demonstrate Your Dedication

Words

"We should go on vacation together next year."

"I want to be with you forever."

"I want to spend the rest of my life with you."

"I'm devoted to you."

"You're the one for me."

"I can't imagine my life without you."

"I care deeply about you."

Talk about your future together

Use "we" and "our" instead of "I" and "my"

Talk about getting married, having
children, and growing old together

Actions

Wear a ring
(a promise, engagement, or wedding ring)

Hold hands and use other
public displays of affection

Invite your partner to leave his/her
personal items at your house

Become an exclusive couple

Stand up for your mate in front of others

Introduce your mate to
your family and friends

Get a pet together

Be faithful and don't flirt with other people

Get engaged or married

Plan a vacation together

Treat your mate with respect,
even when he/she is not around

In addition to offering assurances about your relationship (i.e. demonstrating your togetherness, stressing your commitment, implying that your relationship has a future, and showing your faithfulness), it is also very important to always tell and retell your partner how much you love him or her. This may sound trivial, but failing to express your love can actually result in your partner feeling devalued, unwanted, and just plain down in the dumps.

But, you don't always have to say something verbally to your partner to express your love. One of my favorite things about Hus is that other people notice how much he loves me. My friends and family have said on several occasions over the last 11 plus years, "He looks at you like you're still teenagers." They're right. He does.

> "Being verbally and physically expressive about our feelings for each other frequently is very important to us. With the busyness of life, this can easily be pushed aside- but it's important to be mindful of doing that on a day-to-day basis... and squeezing it in whenever we can."
>
> -Amanda, in a relationship with Fernando since July 2002 & married since September 2007

CREATIVE ASSURANCES

The real tip here, however, is to keep things interesting by assuring your partner in unique ways. You could call your mate while at work, write your vows on the sidewalk, send an email, leave a note on your partner's car, post a few sweet words on your partner's Facebook wall, text your love message, spell it out on a cake, put a note in your lover's lunch, or just say it in person. Any way that you decide to do it, you will make your partner feel appreciated, significant, and loved by telling him or her every single day.

Hus writes me little love notes. And he's done this on a consistent basis since we began dating over 11 years ago. For example, 9 or 10 years ago, he bought me a CD (remember those?), opened it, and took out the little booklet that came in the case (you know, with info about the artist). He proceeded to write a very long love letter with a black permanent marker in the entire booklet. The sweetest part was that he used many of the song titles and lyrics from that CD for inspiration. It was amazing. And while the long-love-letter-writing has slowed down a bit in recent years, he still leaves me little love notes all over the place. In fact, I currently have a piece of ripped paper taped to the inside of my sun visor in my car that reads, "I heart you Dream Girl." I love him for stuff like that.

Need some help being more creative in your love declarations? Take a look below for 13 ways to say those three little words.

13 Ways to Say "I Love You"

I'm infatuated with you.

I cherish you.

143.
(that one's for my friend Ashley)

You're my everything.

You are my soul mate.

I'm passionate about you.

I'm better because of you.

You are my life.

You are my sunshine.

You set my heart on fire.

I've been looking for you my entire life.

I want to be with you always.

I heart the hell out of you.

Another great way to express your romantic feelings is to take five minutes out of each day to write a brief journal entry (anything from one sentence to an entire page) about why you love your partner. Maybe it was something that your partner did or said that made you want to write. Or maybe your partner didn't do anything, but instead, you just feel the urge to profess your love on paper. Whatever the reason, keeping a love journal can easily benefit you and your relationship.

Journaling about your partner can help you better appreciate him or her, and if you ever decide to share this journal with your mate, the experience can bring you closer as a couple and enhance feelings of intimacy between the two of you. Also, if you ever feel like you've been fighting way too much, looking back at your love journal can sometimes rekindle feelings you once had and hopefully make you realize what's truly important. Interestingly, research has shown that writing down affectionate thoughts about your loved ones can actually reduce your cholesterol![76] So, what are you waiting for? Start journaling today!

♥

If you feel it, then say it. Tell your partner how you feel about your relationship every single day. Don't let a day go by where you miss an opportunity to declare your love or show your commitment. When Hus spoke those sweet words to me on our wedding day, he was not only expressing his commitment and love to me, but he was also suggesting that our relationship had a future, a long future. And every day since then, we both have continued to demonstrate our dedication to one another by offering assurances and saying "I love you" in unique ways.

"After 40 years, we express our love for each other when we hold hands or with words or with subtle ordinary things like offers of help or words of concern or just being there for each other in times of stress or need."

-Debby, married to John since December 1970

CHAPTER nine: add in a dash of spice

Almost every weekend, Hus and I make waffles. We love waffles! And, making them together on a regular basis is a predictable part of our life that we both highly enjoy. He knows that I'll put the waffle maker and other ingredients on the counter, and I know that he'll mix the ingredients and actually make the waffles. We are both able to predict how the morning will play out. Every once in awhile, however, we'll spice things up by making cinnamon rolls or French toast or sausage and eggs in lieu of waffles. This novelty tends to keep our Sunday mornings interesting.

Although the above personal example may seem a bit insignificant in the grand scheme of things, the fact of the matter is that many couples struggle to find a balance between their need for stability and their desire for excitement. This relational tension has been referred to by researchers, like Dr. Leslie Baxter, Ph.D., of the University of Iowa, as the novelty vs. predictability dialectic.[77] When individuals are involved in any romantic relationship, there's a lot of comfort that comes with being able to know what's going to happen next. On the other hand, *always* knowing what's next can become extremely dull and boring. The key is to find a happy medium between the two extremes.

THE NEED FOR STABILITY

At some level, we all want to know what's going to happen next. Many of us are simply impatient by nature and others are just curious about the future. Our interest in the future spans the immediate, trivial, distant, and serious. We want to know if it's going to rain this weekend, if we're making the right decisions, and even when we're going to die.

And, our interest in the future carries over into our love lives. We all like the security that comes with being able to predict how our partners will react in certain situations and how our relationships will progress (i.e. whether they will successfully continue or tragically end). We want to know how our life with this person will play out. But it's not *just* about the distant future. We also like to know about how our day-to-day life together will unfold.

It's nice to know that on Wednesday nights, Hus and I watch *The Middle* and *Modern Family* together while (occasionally) folding laundry. I look forward to it every week. That kind of consistency in our schedule brings me great comfort. I also like to be able to say that I can safely rely on Hus for absolutely anything. Knowing that he will always be there for me also adds consistency to my life.

Having a routine and being able to rely on another human being is soothing and allows people to trust others, find security in their own and in their shared life, and empowers individuals to become more confident in the success of their romantic relationships.

Several researchers[78] have argued that rituals are a foundational characteristic of marriage. And this makes sense as many of you were raised to value rituals and routines. In fact, studies have shown that rituals strengthen families by increasing the amount of contact among their members,[79] protecting family members from isolation and uncertainty,[80] and helping adolescents develop a sense of identity.[81] So it's completely logical that you would continue to desire this kind of stability in your adult romances as well. Simply put: predictability is comforting.

Imagine being in a relationship where you struggled to figure out what your partner was thinking, where you never knew how your partner would react to bad (or good) news, where you never did the same activity twice, and where you were never sure if your relationship was going well or falling apart. For most of us, this would be a nightmare. As humans we crave reliability. Unfortunately, too much routine and consistency can lead to feelings of boredom, frustration, and dissatisfaction; which is why we also have a strong need for excitement.

THE NEED FOR EXCITEMENT

While it may be obvious to most of you, engaging in novel, amusing, and exciting activities with your partner is **very** beneficial to your relationship. Some of us (like Hus) can get easily bored with the monotony of day-to-day life. And spicing things up with a little excitement here and there is usually an easy fix for these feelings.

Dr. Arthur Aron, Ph.D., of the State University of New York at Stony Brook, and several of his colleagues[82] conducted five studies to thoroughly examine how participating in activities with your partner influences the quality of your relationship.

Studies one and two found a strong positive relationship between participating in new and exciting activities and experienced relationship quality. So, as the activities in your relationship increase in perceived newness and excitement, your experienced relationship quality also tends to increase.

These first two studies were correlational in nature (i.e. the studies showed that the two variables were related, but they did not show which variable caused the other--does increased relationship quality cause people to engage in more exciting activities OR does engaging in more exciting activities cause increased relationship quality?). Because of this, the researchers decided to conduct three more studies to help shed some light on the cause-effect relationship between these two variables.

"John and I try to enjoy a 'Date Night' each week. Sometimes, we go to a nice restaurant for dinner or grab drinks at a local pub. But other times, we stay home and watch movies or play video games together. Regardless of the activity, we try to set aside at least one night each week for the two of us to relax, connect, and enjoy time with each other."

-Lisa, in a relationship with John since 2008 & married since May 2011

The next three studies examined (in a few different ways) the impact that engaging in exciting and not-so-exciting activities has on experienced relationship quality with dating and married couples. All of the studies had couples come to a lab and complete relationship quality surveys prior to engaging in a predetermined activity. All three studies also had couples complete the same set of relationship quality surveys.

The researchers discovered that shared participation in novel and arousing activities, compared with shared participation in mundane activities, increased experienced relationship quality. Interestingly, participants' experienced relationship quality significantly increased after only about 10 minutes of engaging in the new and interesting activity! The take-home message: take an hour or so to plan a few fun, interesting activities with your partner to enhance your relationship quality.

I would venture to say that a lack of excitement, as opposed to a lack of stability, is likely the more common relationship problem. So, what can you do to spice things up a bit? Whether you've been together for 6 months or for 40 years, spending quality time with your partner, especially when that time is spent doing something new and interesting, can help build and maintain your relationship at any stage. Check out these unique date ideas--a few for every season.

4 Fall Date Ideas

Find Your Way Through a Corn Maze
Corn mazes are a ton of fun! But, beware. If both of you are terrible navigators, this may not be the date for you. Follow the map through the corn maze while making it to each checkpoint inside. This is a fun way to see how well you work together as a team to achieve a goal.

Get Scared Together
Find a local haunted house or other haunted attraction (We absolutely LOVE Markoff's haunted forest in Dickerson, MD) and plan a fun night of screaming with your partner. You could end the night with a scary movie cuddled up together.

Carve Pumpkins
This date can be spread out into an all day event. First, look up pumpkin patches. Then, take the long drive out to the country and share your childhood Halloween memories. Once you're there, search for the perfect pumpkin together. You might even want to take a hayride for fun. When you get home, carve your pumpkins while listening to music and planning your costumes for that night in October. Place your pumpkins outside for all to see. If you're extra crafty, get an extra pumpkin from the patch to make homemade pie to share later- it's easier than you think. Google it.

Go for a Walk

Low on cash? Taking a walk with your partner can be just as romantic and fun as any of these other date ideas. Hold hands, walk around your neighborhood, look at the changing leaves together, and talk about your day. Believe me; talking with your partner is one of the best ways to maintain your relationship.

4 Winter Date Ideas

Take a Class

Learning something new together is a great way to build and maintain your relationship. Look up classes being offered to the public at your local community center, university or college, or any other venue that might be offering a class of interest. For example, you may want to check with a nearby arts & crafts store (you may find a pottery seminar or model airplane building workshop), gourmet restaurant (many times, gourmet restaurants offer cooking classes in the morning), or sports complex (you could learn to play hockey together) to see if anything peaks your interest. You could learn a new language, become competent in web design, perfect your dodge ball abilities, or familiarize yourself in the art of poetry. Taking a class together can bring you closer as a couple and give you something to do for a few weeks.

Rent a Classic Romantic Movie

Snuggle up on the couch and watch your favorite romantic movie. *The Notebook*, *Casablanca*, *P.S. I Love You*, *Sleepless in Seattle*, *Titanic*, *The Time Traveler's Wife*, and *Ghost* are all great choices.

Go Tubing

Get bundled up in your cutest snow gear, buy some inner tubes, and spend the day flying down a steep hill with your partner. Better yet, if you live within driving distance of a ski resort that offers tubing as an option, go there. The excitement that you will experience and the mishaps that will likely occur will leave you with a few good stories to share with others down the road. When you're done, split a warm hot chocolate and reminisce about your adventurous day together.

Build a Snowman

Low on cash? If you live in a snowy environment, occupy yourselves by building a snowman (or snow-woman) together. Hey, you could even have a playful snowball fight with your partner.

4 Spring Date Ideas

Pick Fruit

Strawberries and apples and peaches... oh my! Find a U-Pick orchard near you and spend the day perusing the land for the best produce money can buy. Before you go, learn about how to choose the ripest fruit with your mate.

Tour the Town

It doesn't matter whether you live in a small town or the big city, taking a tour of where you live can be really fun for you and your partner. You can either go to your local visitor's bureau or look online for a list of places to go and things to see. For instance, you could look up where the local historical landmarks, art galleries, haunted houses, antique shops, Victorian homes, or museums are located in your town. Make a map of these sights, print out information about each sight, and then you and your mate can spend the day following the map and learning about everything in your neck of the woods.

Pack a Picnic

Make some sandwiches, load up on fruit, grab your favorite beverage, and bring a big blanket. Pick a spot in the shade for you and your mate to eat, relax, talk, and perhaps kiss a little bit. Turn off your cell phones, take in the scenery, and just enjoy each other's company.

Take a Drive

Low on cash? Put a few bucks in the tank and go for a drive. Park somewhere with a great view and make out in the back seat. Regressing to your teenage years will be fun and exciting for both of you. If there's a park nearby, go play on the swings while talking about your life dreams with one another. Maybe you've always wanted to go to Paris or learn Chinese or own a doggy daycare. Whatever it is, sharing your aspirations with your partner will help grow closer as a couple. Been together forever? You may be surprised what you don't know about your partner.

4 Summer Date Ideas

Go to a Fair or Festival
Summer is a great time to go to local fairs and festivals. Take your partner out for an exciting evening filled with rides, cotton candy, funnel cakes, and games. Maybe you could even win them a prize!

Rent a Boat
Whether you go paddle-boating or speedboating, spending the day on a boat in the middle of a lake, river, bay, or ocean is an extremely romantic date where you can get away from it all with your partner. Look up local bodies of water near you and you'll likely find some kind of boat rental nearby. Pack a meal for an added romantic touch.

Watch a Movie Outside
Try to find a local drive-in, any organization that's playing a movie outside, or buy your own outdoor theater, get a few huge blankets, and snuggle up with your partner under the stars.

Star Search
Low on cash? Go online and find a constellation guide. Choose some constellations to find, print out information about each constellation, get a blanket, and lay out under the stars. Search for each constellation while learning about them together.

I know what you're thinking, "how can life **always** be new and exciting?" Well, it doesn't have to be. Instead, spicing up your relationship by doing something new *every once in a while* is a really great thing. Just switching around your daily routine can keep things interesting. Take up a new hobby together, go on vacation, or just change out your regular date night restaurant for an interactive dining experience like a Japanese steakhouse or fondue restaurant. It will be a new experience, and if you've ever been to one of these restaurants before, you know that they're definitely exciting as well.

♥

Whatever activity you decide to do, the important part is that you do it with your partner and that it's new, interesting, and exciting for the both of you. But remember, working towards having a healthy balance between the novelty that we desire and the predictability that we need is what will help to maintain your relationship.

chapter ten:

manage that conflict

"C onflict is an unavoidable fact of life."[83] Everyone does it, few like talking about it, and hardly anyone enjoys it. For decades, researchers have recognized that conversations about conflict are extremely sensitive and rather difficult, and have subsequently discovered a variety of ways to best go about initiating, engaging in, and ending arguments; which can make your life a whole lot easier.

RELATIONAL CONFLICT

When I talk to my students about relational conflict, I always ask them: "What do you think most couples fight about?" Their responses tend to shock me. Not because they're foolish, but because they typically seem to hit the nail on the head. "Money! Kids! Sex!" they shout. I then agree with them and say, "What else?" They look confused. "Chores!" one student yells, while another exclaims, "In-laws!" I reply, "Right and right."

In fact, Paula Hall, a well known Sexual and Relationship Psychotherapist in the U.K., claims that the majority of arguments in romantic relationships tend to center around one of the following five topics: money, sex, work, children, and housework. This makes complete sense to me. I would venture to say that Hus and I generally have at least one disagreement, dispute, or tiff about *each* of these topics every single week! Money, sex, work, children, and housework all have the potential to induce large amounts of stress in any single person, so it only seems natural that they cause quarrels among lovers.

However, as Dr. John Gottman, Ph.D., (that guy I keep referencing—because he's amazing) would say, it's not always about whether or not you *have* conflict with your partner. The key to a successful relationship actually stems from your ability to effectively deal with that conflict. It's also important to note that most problematic issues in marriages (about 69%, in fact) don't ever get *solved*. Instead, the majority of problems are *managed* by romantic partners. This is vital to truly understanding conflict in romantic relationships. Simply having conflict does not mean that your relationship is doomed. Conflict is an essential component of happy, healthy partnerships. It's about how you handle it. If you experience and engage in a significant amount of destructive conflict that demeans, demoralizes, offends, or ignores one or both partners, you need to turn things around before your relationship begins to deteriorate.

As my students and I continue our talk about conflict, we usually discuss **why** people fight about these five popular topics. Below are a few actual answers provided by three of my students in a writing assignment about conflict in romantic relationships. Specifically, they were asked, "Why do you think people fight about sex, money, children, chores, and work as much as they do? Why do these topics consume our conflict interactions?"

"... because they're important! For instance, if you don't have money, then you can't live. Money makes the world go 'round. And when people need it, they go crazy. Crazy people argue a lot."

"... because people get stressed out by all of those things. Figuring out everything about the kids is hard. When they're little, you have to worry about all of the extra chores and when they're older, you have to worry about the discipline stuff. And then when they're teens, you have to actually worry about them and their safety. It's exhausting."

> "... because people have their own way of doing things; they have preconceived notions about how things should and should not happen. And when things don't go your way or happen the way you expected or your partner doesn't act in a way that you want them to, you freak out. You tell your partner that you didn't like what they did (even if it's not really important), you boss your partner around, you tell your partner how they "should" have done it, or you start to feel unhappy about how things are. This leads to conflict."

I have to agree with all of these answers. Money, sex, chores, kids, and work are *important* (they're activities that take up most, if not all, of our time) and *stressful* (especially on those days when you look at your house that hasn't been cleaned for 3 weeks, your kids are running around like Tasmanian Devils, and you can't remember the last time you had a minute alone with your partner). But most of all, I think that we experience a large majority of conflict because of our own particular preferences about life.

Everyone develops their own ideas about how life should (and should not) play out based on how we grew up, what we value, our religious or spiritual beliefs, the media, and our environment. For example, I grew up eating a home-cooked meal just about every night as a child. We rarely went out to eat, ordered in, or picked up fast food. Hus grew up a good part of his life like this, but he also experienced a significant time period (at *least* the second half of his childhood) where he and his family ate out or ordered in on a very regular basis, rarely sharing a meal that was made at home. When Hus and I first started dating, he would take me out to dinner a lot and I thought it was really fun. It was something that I seldom did prior to meeting him. It was new and exciting. But then, I started to realize that this wasn't just Hus trying to woo me. Instead, it was part of his routine. He was accustomed to going out to eat. And I was not. As you can probably guess, this created some conflict in our early relationship. Not a lot of conflict--it's really not that big of a deal. But, it definitely caused a handful of unnecessary disagreements and comments.

Maybe you like to save money and your husband is a bit of a frivolous spender. You're likely going to get into arguments about that 59-inch television that he bought because you think it's a waste of money, especially when you already have a 42-inch television. Who's to say that two ridiculously large televisions in one house are excessive? Okay, I will: it's ridiculous. Sorry.

This problem becomes particularly prevalent when we have children. Stereotypically, mom and dad each cause their own individual set of problems here. Among other things, moms tend to cause a conflict when they engage in gatekeeping and dads tend to cause conflict when they don't pull their own weight.

Let's start with mom. Gatekeeping is when one parent (usually mom) takes control of the care-giving and household chores. She then (either consciously or unconsciously) limits dad's involvement by preventing him from caring for their child ("It's okay, I'll do it"), criticizing how he cares for their child ("That's not how you change a diaper"), or failing to encourage him. Try not to tell your partner how he should or should not care for his child; bite your tongue. He may not have the same knowledge about newborns as you, but he's perfectly capable of figuring it out. Make sure that he knows how much you appreciate him and compliment when he does something well. When you begin your new life as parents by gatekeeping, you set the scene for how the two of you share parenting for years to come. Studies[84] have found that staying away from gatekeeping will not only empower dad to be more involved, but it can also significantly decrease conflict in your relationship. And trust me; you're going to want the least amount of conflict as possible at this time.

Don't worry, I didn't forget about all of the dads out there. For many (but certainly not all) dads, the large number of new duties that come with becoming a parent and the reality that their lifestyle has to seriously change can be a bit overwhelming. Instead of taking a back seat, step up and be equal parents with your baby mama. I understand that this is not physically possible for some because you either work more often than mom or you don't live with mom and baby, but you can still do your part. Remember, you created this baby, too. And, you are just as capable of caring for and raising this baby as mom is. If you're having trouble figuring out what needs to be done, sit down with your mate and talk it out. Discuss each of your strengths and weaknesses (What do you think you're good at and what's difficult for you to handle?) and likes and dislikes (What would you enjoy doing with your child and what would you rather not do?). Then, make a plan about what "your part" and what "her part" entails. Keep in mind that you both may need to do things that you don't like or that you're not particularly good at. Sorry, but this is part of parenting. You'll figure it out.

The child(ren)-induced conflict doesn't end at infancy. As parents, you will both need to continuously check-in with one another about several hundred more child-raising issues over the next 20 or so years. From how to best deal with tantrums to who is going to give your child(ren) "the talk" to managing your teen's hormone-induced outbursts to figuring out how the hell you're going to pay for college, nurturing a child from birth to adulthood is daunting, nerve-racking, and it will test the strength of your relationship. Keep the lines of communication open, anticipate typical child-raising issues, and talk about how you each would like to handle them.

That leaves us with sex (please refer to chapter seven), household chores (please see chapter three), and work. Work can be tricky. Some couples find themselves in a battle of wills about who works harder or about how one partner doesn't work hard enough (which can sometimes lead to unemployment and a whole new set of problems). Other couples fight when one partner spends too much time at work or is continuously working on job-related projects, even when at home. Trying to create a balance between work and home is not easy.

> "I get fed up with him either not doing enough around the house and me feeling like I do everything or that he's procrastinating so much on something that I just can't take it and I get pissy with him."
>
> -Natalia, in a relationship with Colin since January 1998 and married since October 2001

I try to make a conscious effort to balance the time and energy that I put towards my personal life versus my work life. And, I'm *very* motivated to do this. For example, if my writing or teaching begins to suffer, I'll try to socialize less so that I can make more time for it. On the other hand, if I feel like I'm not spending enough time with Hus or with my kiddos, I'll cut back on my workload by taking the day off or saying "no" to new project ideas. I feel like I'm only truly happy when my life is balanced.

A 2008 article entitled, "Navigating personal and relational concerns: The quest for equilibrium" published in the *Journal of Personality and Social Psychology* describes a new theory about how and why we try to achieve this balance that I love so much.[85]

The authors begin by explaining the two domains in their model: relational and personal. Personal concerns involve "behaviors that we enact for ourselves to gratify self-oriented needs and promote self-oriented goals,"[86] while relational concerns involve "behaviors that we enact for our relationships to gratify relationship-oriented needs and promote relationship-oriented goals."[87] Basically, we're either concerned with things having to do with ourselves (like working, making money, improving our own competence, declaring our independence, or exercising) or with things having to do with our relationships with others (like improving intimacy, engaging in sexual activities, talking with loved ones, or spending time with our friends). So for example, when I spend time writing on my blog, I'm satisfying my personal needs and when Hus and I discuss our daily activities with one another, I'm satisfying my relational needs.

The researcher's *Personal-Relational Equilibrium Model* argues that when individuals don't have a good balance between their relational and personal domains, they want to restore that balance by enacting certain behaviors to achieve equilibrium. Furthermore, if individuals can't restore balance, they experience reduced life satisfaction and reduced physical, psychological, and relational well-being. All of this dissatisfaction can easily cause conflict between partners. To test their model, the researchers conducted four studies, each of which examined their model in a different way. The researchers discovered that (1) individuals are highly motivated to fix anticipated disequilibrium, that they think they will experience in the future, by finding balance, (2) individuals report low life satisfaction and well-being during times of unbalance, (3) individuals have a high motivation to restore balance and actually enact behaviors to do so in the days after disequilibrium is realized, and (4) individuals who experience balance between their relational and personal domains experience more physical and relational well-being, higher life satisfaction, and less depression and anxiety than those who experience disequilibrium.

In the end, we all want balance in our lives. The inability to maintain that balance can result in anxiety, depression, low life satisfaction, reduced happiness in our relationships, and more conflict within our relationships. Unfortunately, in our society, the relational domain is what tends to be neglected. Americans value their jobs and autonomy so much, that we sometimes forget what's truly important in life: our relationships with other people.

The next time you're spending too much time at the office or taking on way too many projects at school, take a break and do something fun with the one you love so that maybe you can begin to restore your equilibrium.

In addition to recognizing the top five spat topics (money, sex, chores, work, and children) and attempting to deal with them effectively, we should also become familiar with and try to manage what researcher Dr. Leslie A. Baxter, Ph.D., has named *relational dialectics* (a.k.a. tensions in a relationship that are caused by the different wants and needs of each partner).

DIALECTICAL TENSIONS

During her extensive examination of relationships and the tensions that accompany them, Dr. Baxter and several of her colleagues over the years have identified four main dialectics: autonomy vs. togetherness, openness vs. closedness, masculine vs. feminine gender roles, and novelty vs. predictability (which was discussed in chapter nine and therefore will not be discussed here).

AUTONOMY VS. TOGETHERNESS

We all have the desire to be around other people, especially our significant others. When we first start dating someone, we usually can't think of doing anything else but spending every waking moment with our new love interest. However, we can sometimes feel overwhelmed or even like we're being smothered by our relationship when we spend *too* much time together. This relational tension has been referred to as the *autonomy versus togetherness dialectic*.[88]

The more time you spend together, the greater your need for independence usually becomes, which can produce stress in your relationship. Problems can also arise when people don't spend enough time with each other. What can you do to manage this tension with your partner?

First, be sure to never assume that your partner will automatically want to hang out with you, and only you, all of the time. People need their space. You may think that spending every free moment with your partner will bring you closer together. But, too much

"I think one thing that is necessary for a happy marriage is a balance of time spent together developing mutual interests and time spent apart exploring individual interests and developing friendships with others. I really like learning things from John and telling him about things that really interest me. And, I like that we have time apart to refresh and then time together to share things with each other and to enjoy other things together."

-Rebecca, in a relationship with John since September 2003 and married since August 2006 togetherness can actually create stress in your relationship and can even drive the two of you apart.

"We try to spend time alone together whenever we can— we take walks, go out for coffee, go out to dinner."

-Debby, married to John since December 1970

Second, make sure that you both have your own separate activities and your own separate groups of friends. This will help each of you feel independent and will likely help you to better appreciate the time that you actually spend together. To be happy in life, you need to have your own individual identities.

On the other hand, relationships take a lot of work. You can't build a relationship solely on text messages or phone calls. You need to spend face-to-face time together where you learn about each other and do things that *both* of you like to do. You can do this by making the time that you spend together *quality* time. Do some fun and interesting activities instead of always watching television or going to the same restaurant together. And once your relationship starts to take shape, it is necessary that you begin to build an identity for your relationship (while maintaining your own individual identities). You can do this by developing shared attitudes, activities, or interests ("our song" or "our restaurant"), identifying relationship-specific likes and dislikes ("We love Chinese food."), and creating an insider language. An insider language? I know what you're thinking: "I have to create a new language with my partner? WTF?" No, you don't have to actually create a brand new language. Instead, couples who have been around one another long enough are able to communicate in a way that other people cannot always comprehend. For instance, a few times a week, Hus will come home, I'll ask him "How was your day?" and he'll respond with "The usual." He doesn't have to elaborate for me to completely understand what he means—he had to deal with the same bullshit that he always has to deal with at work, he hates his job, and he wishes that he could quit. Insider language could also include a phrase that the two of you use in certain situations to mean something completely different from the phrase's actual meaning. For example, you may say "We've got to get the oil changed in our car soon" when you want to leave a party without anyone else catching on. Insider language is a sign of a healthy relationship. In fact, researchers have found evidence to support the notion that using insider language can enhance satisfaction, reduce conflict, and strengthen the bond that the two of you share. As stated by Jamie Turndoff, Ph.D.

and New York City relationship therapist, "Using made-up language is an easy way to inject positive communication into everyday life."

This relational tension is not just about time spent together and understanding one another. It's also about being emotionally reliant vs. self-sufficient. Becoming too dependent on your partner can also create stress or arguments in your relationship. While some dependence is warranted and expected in serious relationships (it *is* important to rely on your partner), relying on your partner for everything can become cumbersome and make your partner feel underappreciated or taken advantage of. Be aware of this tension the next time you want your partner to help you with something. Could you do it by yourself? Do you really need your partner to help you?

Create emotional bonds with your partner without smothering. Spend quality time together and periodic time apart. And communicate in a way that develops your oneness without actually becoming one person. Learning how to balance this tension, and the remaining tensions below, is extremely important for every successful relationship.

OPENNESS VS. CLOSEDNESS

In addition to finding a balance between autonomy and togetherness, we must also figure out how to manage our innate desire to share information about *ourselves* while continuing keeping some things private. We also want to share things about *our partners* and *our relationship* with other people, while maintaining a certain level of discretion. This is called the *openness versus closedness dialectic.*[89]

In order to build a relationship with another person, we have to be willing to openly convey our feelings and reveal ourselves to them. But when we do this, we make ourselves vulnerable to scrutiny. So we may try to spread out our self-disclosures over time or limit the expression of our feelings. As you probably have guessed, this can cause serious tension and even conflict in relationships. For example, some of you may disclose in large quantities and therefore expect others to do the same. If your partner fails to reciprocate, you may feel like your partner is not interested in building a bond with you. Oppositely, some of you may feel overwhelmed with your partner who tells you every single little thing that he or she is feeling, in great detail, every single day. You really need to be in tune with your partner. Pay attention to cues sent by him or her and figure out what an appropriate level of openness entails. You could also have a direct, verbal discussion about it. Ask your mate, "Does my self-disclosure make you uncomfortable? What would you be comfortable with?" If you feel like you're disclosing too much or too little or if you sense that your mate is unhappy with your self-disclosure, manage that tension by changing your communication practices or by talking to your mate about it.

Once you've discovered how to best self-disclose within your relationship (so that you don't offend, embarrass, overwhelm, or shock your partner), you need to also assess your disclosure habits to individuals outside of your relationship.

I can clearly remember a time when the importance of balancing this tension was revealed to me. A few years ago, Hus, our kids, and I traveled to the east coast from Indiana to visit family for the holidays. Near the beginning of our trip, my mom made a comment to Hus about something he had told me a week earlier. I didn't think anything about the conversation that ensued between my mom and myself, but apparently Hus did.

Hus later pulled me to the side and said, "You told *your mom* about *that?*" To which I replied, "Yeah, I talk to my mom about everything." "EVERYTHING?!" he yelled. "Maybe not *everything*, but most stuff," I said. Hus looked at me and answered, "Well, I'd appreciate it if we could keep our private conversations a little more private."

After our discussion, I began to think about why this act upset him. Then I remembered a communication theory that may be able to shed some light on the cause of our exchange.

Dr. Sandra Petronio, Ph.D., Professor of Communication Studies at Indiana University-Purdue University Indianapolis, developed a theory known as communication privacy management (CPM), which addresses the tension between sharing and concealing private information in disclosure situations.[90] CPM is a rule-based theory, which explains that individuals develop boundary and privacy rules that help them decide whether to reveal or conceal private information about themselves or about their significant others. These rules are made to help individuals maximize rewards and avoid any costs associated with self-disclosure. Central to CPM is the notion that a person "owns" information about him or herself until he or she shares it with someone else, at which point, the information becomes co-owned by both people. Also, if boundary or privacy rules are violated, disclosers could feel anger, distrust, or distain towards the person they shared their private information with.

There are five main principles used to explain how people control whether information about themselves or about their relationship partners is kept secret or shared.

- First, individuals believe that they own their private information about themselves.

- Second, individuals therefore believe that they have the right to control whether or not the information is shared with others.

- Third, individuals use privacy rules that they have developed to decide whether they will open a privacy boundary (i.e. share the information) or keep the boundary closed (i.e. not share the information).

- The fourth principle states that when individuals share their private information with others, those other people become shareholders of that information. It is assumed that these new owners of the private information will also follow privacy rules that were developed by one or both people.

- The last principle is concerned with what happens when rules are broken. Specifically, when a problem occurs (e.g. the privacy rules are broken), individuals may begin to not trust the person they shared information with. This could subsequently lead to suspicion or uncertainty when deciding whether to share information with this individual again in the future.

When individuals self-disclose, they're expressing something (private information) that they feel belongs to them, and therefore, they feel that they should retain the right to control it, even after the initial disclosure. Thus, rules about when and how to share information with others are created by the initial information-holder prior to the initial disclosure and then again after that individual has shared his or her information. The rules that are developed can be the same and stable over time through repeated use or can also be highly situational and may be changed to fit new circumstances. These rules help people know when to conceal information, when to reveal information, what type of information can be revealed, and to whom the information can be revealed.

To go back to my example, Hus had private information that he shared with me. When Hus decided to tell me this information, he had the opportunity to also give me some rules about who else can and cannot hear the information. These rules would have helped me know what is and what is not acceptable when discussing or sharing Hus' private information. But since Hus didn't directly provide me with a set of rules, I was unaware that talking to my mom about it would be offensive to him.

This is partly due to Hus' lack of directions, but it's mostly due to the fact that I broke an unwritten rule that Hus and I (and many other people) have in our marriage—some things are meant to be between the two of us and no one else. The hard part here is determining what information should be kept private and what information can be revealed to others. Unless it is explicitly stated, you may find this task to be rather difficult. Talk with your partner on a regular basis about this subject. And when your mate tells you something mildly private, it's probably best to err on the side of safety and keep your lips sealed.

After thinking about this myself, I've decided that the next time Hus tells me something that he considers private information, I won't be telling my mom. (Well, I'll at least make sure that she doesn't say anything about it to Hus this time! Just kidding...kind of.)

MASCULINE VS. FEMININE GENDER ROLES

We all come into relationships with ideas about how men and women should and should not behave and communicate. For instance, in some circles, it's considered inappropriate for men to be emotional and it's expected for women to cry at the drop of a hat. Additionally, some people believe that women should stay at home and be primary caregivers for their children, while men should go to work and provide for their families. It's not my purpose here to tell you which gender roles are good or bad, right or wrong, or appropriate or inappropriate. Instead, I just want you to recognize how important it is that as a couple, you come to a certain level of agreement on this issue. If you and your mate disagree about who should fill each role in your life together, you will likely experience a significant amount of conflict down the road. This relational tension is known as the *gender role dialectic*.[91]

Gender roles can be defined as a set of behaviors and characteristics that are considered appropriate and acceptable for each gender in a given society. These roles are learned. As we grow up, we learn about how we should behave based on our biological sex from various sources like the media, our parents, and our friends. This is why some people follow very strict, traditional gender roles (i.e. men act in one way and women in another) and others seem to cross gender role boundaries in everything they do. Gender roles also affect our beliefs about ourselves. They help us to feel valued, worthy, important, and they empower us to achieve our goals. For example, if a woman wants to go to college, but she has always learned that a woman's role is not in education, but at home with the kids, her dreams of an education will likely be stifled by her fear of breaking a gender role that has been engrained in her since she was little. On the other hand, many women happily comply with traditional female roles. Not because they feel like it is their only choice, but because they know that they actually have a choice. And, staying at home is the choice that they have made. Either way, it's clear that gender roles significantly impact our way of life with the opposite sex.

Probably the most prominent issue within this tension involves figuring out how the work-load of life is going to be divided. Some couples want to align with traditional gender roles (man works while woman tends to the home and children), others opt for a more modern lifestyle (man and woman both work, tend to children, and take care of home together), and still others decide that a more unconventional way of life works for them (woman works and man tends to home and children). Whatever you and your partner decide to do here is not the concern. As I said, the point is that you and your mate should hold similar values about this, or conflict will most likely occur. If you fundamentally want your life to be one way and your mate expects your life to be another way, someone is going to get the short end of the stick and resentment will eventually build up.

In order to really understand gender roles and to subsequently learn about how to manage them, I think it's important to more deeply discuss their origin. This may be difficult for some to believe, but studies have shown that famous television couples, along with other aspects of the media, have a significant impact on how we choose our mates, communicate and interact with each other, and view sex in our relationships.[92] When in a relationship, we all use various prototypes (idealized visions of the perfect relationship) to compare to our own relationship. We do this to see if the connection with our significant other measures up to our prototype(s). Many of the relationship prototypes we use for comparison are found in the media, which heavily rely on gender role stereotypes to determine how romantic partners will behave and what they will or will not say to one another.

Numerous problems can arise when we use these television and film relationships as prototypes in our lives. From men believing that women should keep up their appearances but that men don't have to do the same (Think about it: Marge Simpson is more attractive than Homer, Louis Griffin is more attractive than Peter, and even Wilma Flintstone is more attractive than Fred. Okay, so those are all cartoons, but what about the couples on *Married with Children*, *King of Queens*, *Fresh Prince of Bel-Air*, and *Everybody Loves Raymond*? The females are all beautiful and/or skinny and the men are all overweight and/or less-than-attractive.), to women believing that a wife is destined to nag everyone in her family every single day of her life (Think: *Malcolm in the Middle*, *Desperate Housewives*, and *Roseanne*), typical relationships found in the media create a skewed perception of the dynamics of relationships in the real world.

Even if you think that the media doesn't affect you, gender role stereotypes (which are passed down from generation to generation as well) can still influence the way you interact with your significant other. And, they can cause serious damage to your relationship (by way of lowered satisfaction and unnecessary conflict) if and when they take a turn for the worse and begin to consume your relationship.

The second step (the first step being recognizing their origin) to managing gender role stereotypes (especially the negative ones that can hurt your relationship) is to become aware of them. Here are 4 female gender role stereotypes and 4 male gender role stereotypes that are commonly relied on when in relationships.

4 Stereotypical Female Roles

Women should (and can easily) manipulate men. Quit treating your man like he's stupid. In the media, men (especially husbands) are often portrayed in a not-so-intelligent manner (think: Al Bundy from *Married with Children* & Doug from *King of Queens*). This is quite unfortunate. And, it adds to our perceptions of how women are supposed to treat the men in their lives. Men are not stupid. Men are not simpleminded. Men are not easily tricked and manipulated. Treating your man like an idiot will not only perpetuate this terrible stereotype, but it will also negatively impact his self-esteem. You do not want to be responsible for that.

Women are supposed to mold a man. Accept your partner for who he is, not for you want him to be. Nobody is perfect. Hey, even you're not perfect. Acknowledging his flaws and liking him anyway is the definition of ***true love***. You cannot change another human being. People have to change on their own. If you really don't like something about your partner and you can't seem to see past it, then maybe he is not the one for you. You have to be able to accept him for who he is. You will be miserable trying to make your relationship work because of who you think he will become one day.

Women are supposed to nag. This has to be stopped! Bossing him around, nagging him to do things, and telling him what he should or should not be doing emasculates him and makes you look like a total bitch (sorry, but it does). He's a grown-ass adult. Roseanne Connor is not a wife you should be emulating. Men don't need you to be their mothers. And, you will be sorry down the road when you have two kids under the age of 5 and one that's 35 going on 12. Believe me, it will not be good.

The woman is in charge. Let go of your desire to control every aspect of the relationship and your life together. You don't need to do everything. I know, many women feel like they *have* to do everything, but the great news is that you don't. There's another **adult** in your relationship, remember? **He's an adult.** Like you, he's also perfectly capable of handing the bills or taking the kids to all of their after-school activities or organizing your vacation next summer or not working and staying home with the kids or even choosing the reception location for your wedding. Think about it: why would you be with him in the first place if he was incompetent? Leading the lives Marie Barone from *Everybody Loves Raymond* or June Cleaver from *Leave it to Beaver* is not the way it has to be. You can share the household duties, child-raising, and control. Really, you can.

4 Stereotypical Male Roles

Men are not emotional or expressive. This is an extremely unfortunate stereotype. Men, you are not cold-hearted, dispassionate, detached individuals (think: Al Bundy from *Married with Children* or Tony from *The Sopranos*). You have feelings. You are sensitive. Sadly, there's just a lot of social pressure on you to *not* express yourself. It's okay. You can tell us how you feel. You even show us how you feel. It's okay, really.

A man should find a super-model wife. I'm not sure how much more clear I can be when I say that contrary to what you see on television and in the movies, ALL WOMEN ARE NOT BEAUTY QUEENS. Real women in the real world do not look like Megan Fox or Angelina Jolie. Don't get me wrong, there are plenty of gorgeous women in the real world. I guess I just want you to realize that the relationships you see on television (where the woman is hot and the man is, well, not) are not indicative of relationships in real life. Most people are happy with significant others who are of similar attractiveness to themselves. So, quit looking for Gabrielle Solis (*Desperate Housewives*), Lorelai Gilmore (*Gilmore Girls*), or Elena Delgado (*Without a Trace*).

The man is in charge. Like many women, you also need to learn to let go of your desire to control every aspect of the relationship and your life together. When you committed yourself to your significant other, you two became part of the same team. Equal parts of the same team. There's no captain here. You don't need to make all of the decisions yourself, especially the big ones. The media often shows men making huge (and small) decisions without ever consulting their mates (think: Bill Henrickson on *Big Love* or Tony from *The Sopranos*). Making decisions *together* will empower your partner, take some of the weight off of your shoulders, and strengthen the bond that the two of you share.

The man should be the sole provider. This male stereotype is slowly disappearing, but there is still a lot of work to do. Men, if your wife or girlfriend works more often or makes more money than you, it does not make you any less of a man. As long as you contribute to the relationship in other ways (household duties, childcare, emotional support, etc.), you are just as valuable to your relationship as your wife or girlfriend is. It only becomes a problem when you don't work as often as your partner _and_ you don't contribute in other ways. Moving towards a more equal relationship with your significant other will greatly increase you and your partner's satisfaction. You don't need to be the sole provider and your wife does not need to be the primary caregiver. If you each can learn to share both worlds, both of your lives could be a lot easier.

What can you do about all of this? Well, the first step in any 12-step program is to recognize that there is a problem. Be cognizant of your behaviors as you're enacting them. Also, be mindful of certain situations that cause you to behave in these stereotypical ways. Once you've accepted that you play one or more of these cliché gender roles, you can start developing your goals for change. What do you want your new life to look like? Begin thinking about what you can do to achieve your goals. Then, modify your behaviors. You can do this by eliminating the negative behaviors you used to enact (i.e. being in control of everything) and incorporating new positive behaviors in their place (i.e. asking your partner for help with something). Since it generally takes about 21 days (or 3 weeks) to break an undesirable habit or to create a desirable one, you should remove your old actions and insert new ones EVERYDAY for AT LEAST 3 full weeks. This will definitely help you break free of these damaging gender role stereotypes.

For those not-so-damaging gender roles, there are several steps you can take to manage any tension you experience. First, as soon as you think it is appropriate for your relationship, have a talk about which roles you each expect to take on (child-raising, bread-winning, etc). To help the two of you understand each other, you can also discuss why you have your opinions about gender-specific roles. Second, if you feel like your gender role values or beliefs are changing at any point in your relationship, make sure that you talk to your partner about it. It's okay to change your mind. But be prepared to compromise. You may not be able to make a complete role change in your life years after your initial discussion. The change may need to be gradual, especially if it's a big change.

Hus and I didn't get engaged until we were about seven years into our relationship. We began dating in 2000, were engaged and married in 2007, and had our twins in 2009. When we first started talking about marriage around year two, I told Hus that I would take his last name. Jennifer Nicole Gill would become Jennifer Nicole Rosier. It was how I was raised. And, it was how Hus was raised. Women took the last names of their husbands. The end.

Then I grew up a little more and began to question why women had to change their names, but men didn't. It actually started to anger me. Why do *I* have to get rid of *my* name (a name that I've had for 25+ years) and a man gets to keep his? I started rethinking my original promise to Hus. And I felt bad about it. But why? Why did I feel bad about not wanting to change my name? It's *my name*! It's what people have called me my entire life!

But at the end of the day, I felt bad. So I decided to talk to Hus about it. And I was right to feel bad. Hus was not happy about the prospect of me keeping my name. He wasn't angry; he was hurt and uncomfortable. He saw it as a disruption in our union and to be honest, he was uneasy about going against society's marriage grain. But I didn't want to lose my identity, which is what I felt was going to happen.

So, I thought about the alternatives. I could hyphenate. Jennifer Nicole Gill-Rosier didn't sound too bad, but it was really long. I could legally be Jennifer Nicole Rosier and then academically be Jennifer Nicole Gill. But that would have been too confusing. Then I thought about just making my maiden name my new middle name: Jennifer Gill Rosier. I liked it. I brought my idea to Hus and he liked it, too. It was a nice compromise. I felt like I got to keep some of my identity and he felt like I was connected to him and more motivated to be married. And we were both happy that we were willing and able to compromise.

Figuring out how to manage these tensions in your relationship is not easy. But, learning about the things that couples argue about the most and the tools needed for constructive conflict can help you have more successful disagreements with your mate.

CONSTRUCTIVE CONFLICT

Conflict usually occurs when two or more people have differing goals. Maybe one or both people don't agree about the importance or value of said goal(s), or maybe one person is trying to interfere with the attainment of said goal(s). When people decide to deal with conflict, they tend to do so constructively or destructively. Constructive conflict involves cooperation, support, flexibility, compromise or negotiation, and de-escalation.[93] Conversely, destructive conflict is characterized by competition, inflexibility, escalation, domination, defensiveness, and cross complaining.

"We usually go in separate rooms and cool off. Then after a decent amount of time has gone by, we rationally talk about the problem (without attitude) and then we move on. Usually works until the sink is full of dishes again (just kidding!)"

-Steph, in a relationship with Tony since December 2000 and married since October 2009

One of these is clearly easier than the other. Destructiveness doesn't take a whole lot of effort on your part. It's easy to become defensive, to try and dominate a conversation, or to be stubborn and stand your ground no matter what is said. But, constructive conflict is far better for you and your relationship. Below are a few tips for engaging in constructive conflict interactions.

LAY OFF THE CRITICISM
AND LEARN TO COMPLAIN

Unfortunately, many relationships are consumed by criticism. Whether you're consistently knocking how your partner does the laundry, slamming your partner's daily choice of clothing, or always pointing out your partner's inability to be on time (sorry Hus), criticism is a nasty communication technique that, when built up over time, can seriously damage your relationship.

It's important to note that there's a difference between complaining about your partner's actions and criticizing your partner's character. Where complaints can sometimes be helpful (allowing people to take note and possibly make a change), criticisms tend to attack a person's disposition by blaming and generalizing the issue beyond the behavior in question. For instance, "I felt like you didn't support me yesterday when I was sad" is an example of a complaint; while "You never support me" would be an example of criticism. Using words like "always" and "never" represent a critical remark. Try to remove those terms from your vocabulary when talking about the actions of your partner.

Researchers agree with the idea that criticism tends to have negative outcomes. In fact, criticism has been linked to feelings of embarrassment[94] and lower relationship satisfaction[95] within the person being criticized. Furthermore, when comparing communication patterns of happy and unhappy couples, researchers have discovered that distressed couples tend to exhibit more negative verbal behaviors like sarcasm and criticism than happier couples.[96] Dr. John Gottman has even named criticism as one of his "Four Horseman of the Apocalypse" when talking about the four signs which can reveal that couples are headed for break-up or divorce (defensiveness, contempt, and stonewalling being the other three).[97]

How can you change your critical ways? According to Dr. John Gottman and Nan Silver,[98] learning to **complain** more effectively may be able to take the place of criticism. Effective complaining involves identifying **one** specific behavior by your partner that you are unhappy with and not allowing yourself to generalize the issue beyond the behavior in question. However, you still don't want to complain all of the time. Quit your pickin', learn to complain more effectively, and your relationship can be more satisfying.

Defensiveness is usually a response people have during conflict where they shift the blame to someone or something else, whine about what is being said to them, offer more complaints and criticism to their partners, or make excuses for their behaviors. Instead of becoming defensive, individuals in healthy relationships will accept a complaint from a partner and try to work towards a solution. Remember, your partner is coming to you for a reason. And sometimes, it's difficult for us to figure out why our mate would be upset about something. In these situations, it's important for you to listen and try to understand your partner's point of view.

To avoid defensiveness, Dr. John Gottman offers a few steps. First, when your mate is initiating conflict with you, try to be calm. Getting excited or angered won't help the situation. Second, listen to what your mate is saying. If you listen carefully, you'll probably be able to understand what your partner is actually upset about. Lastly, try to respond non-defensively. Drs. Gottman and Silver argue, "we need to ignore what's being said about us and learn to hear our partner's negativity as an attempt to underline how strongly she or he feels about the problem and what desperate measures are being employed to get us to pay attention."[99]

Stop avoiding the conflict by becoming defensive. Own up to your faults (even if you don't always agree) and try to make things better.

> "We take a break and I am usually really quiet. After a while, we both realize how crazy we are being and we talk about the situation. In our last fight, our icebreaker was 'I hope that there are no more tantrums with you or Carter (their son) today.' Then, we both decided to talk to each other with more respect.
>
> -Brandy, in a relationship with Iad since December 1999 and married since October 2003

QUIT YELLING AND
DE-ESCALATE

While most arguments don't usually *begin* as a screaming match, many end up that way. In fact, many disagreements (but certainly not all) start off about seemingly insignificant topics or at the least begin with partners behaving in a civil manner--speaking calmly, at an average rate and volume, and using acceptable language. Sadly, arguments can quickly escalate and turn into larger-than-life wars between romantic partners where yelling, name-calling, insulting, and criticism are common. The fact of the matter is that *any* argument where escalation takes place (and de-escalation does not) is considered destructive.

If you're in an argument with your partner and you can see that things are getting out of hand, there's still hope. You can simply turn conflict around by learning how to de-escalate the conversation. Below are a few statements that you can make to attempt to de-escalate your feud.

"Okay, let's take a 10 minute (or 10 hour) break,
cool down, and then work towards actually solving this problem."

Stepping away from a disagreement, taking a break, and coming back to the issue at a later date (FYI: you have to come back to it) allows people to calm down and think about what they really want to talk about. Many times, people are able to better organize their thoughts and express their feelings more effectively after taking a break. But beware; continuously tabling a discussion is not a good idea. You have to eventually work it out. And, sooner is better than later.

"Wait a minute. What are we really fighting about?"

At times, it's vital that you ask yourself (and your partner) this exact question. Couples have a tendency to engage in what I like to call *cryptic arguing* where they seem to be arguing about one topic when, in fact, they are really upset about something totally unrelated. For instance, you might be angry at your partner about comments made by him or her a week earlier. Instead of talking about how those comments made you feel, you become easily agitated when your mate leaves his or her dirty clothes on the floor. You erupt in anger about the clothes when it's really about the comment made a week prior. Or, you might not be mad at your mate at all. Maybe you're stressed out at work or with the kids and you take it out on your partner for something rather trivial. I think that this happens a lot with couples who have children. For instance, when our twins were infants, Hus and I would argue about the most ridiculous things. "Don't put your soda on the f-ing table! You're going to leave a stain! You always do shit like that!" And that wasn't all. "Why can't you figure this out? It's like you're not even trying" was another fav phrase of ours. At a certain point during these conflicts, one of us would sometimes ask, "What the hell are we really fighting about? Why are we so upset about this?" Saying something like this in a light-hearted tone can easily break the tension during an impassioned quarrel.

"I love you, and you love me. Why are we talking to each other like this?"

Insults, name-calling, negative sarcasm, and other forms of contempt are commonplace in many disagreements between romantic partners. Reiterating your love for one another can put your conversation in perspective. I know when Hus and I have used this strategy, one of the next sentences is something like, "You're right. I don't want to fight with you. I'm sorry." And then we're able to think more rationally and work through the issue. If you really love someone, that kind of hurtful language should not be part of your relationship vocabulary to begin with. But if it sneaks in somehow, you can quickly nip those detrimental conversations in the bud (and de-escalate your conflict) by shifting the focus of your discussion. Emphasizing your love can cause you and your partner to quit using cruel language, remember that you actually care for one another, and maybe even help you solve your problems.

PICK YOUR BATTLES

One of the better pieces of advice given to me by my mom is that whenever you're in a relationship, it's important to pick your battles. Relationships aren't any fun when you're arguing or picking on each other all of the time.

Learning to complain instead of criticize can help with this, but complaining all of the time doesn't really help either. For instance, Hus is late to *everything*. And, since I've always been someone who is on time (i.e. 10 minutes early) to everything, this characteristic of his really irked me. Overtime however, I realized that criticizing his constant lateness was not only hurting our relationship by creating unnecessary conflict, but it wasn't making him any more punctual either. This was a battle that I did not want to have for the rest of my life. I can't say that I've *completely* ignored this pet-peeve of mine, but I definitely don't bring it up as often as I once did. It's just not worth it. And, I've learned to complain more about specific instances where his tardiness has seriously affected me instead of criticizing him as a person. Think about the many insignificant battles that you and your mate have and try to cut out a few of them.

♥

Overall, conflict should play a role in your relationship. It's inevitable. You will argue. You will fight. You might even say things you don't mean. But in the end, you need to be willing to acknowledge and respect your mate's point of view and try to work toward a solution in a loving, supportive, flexible way.

LISTEN

Listening is powerful. Being listened to can make you feel loved and appreciated, or it can make you feel disrespected and unimportant when your messages are neglected. Feeling like you're truly listened to can bring people together, while a lack of listening from your partner can tear the two of you apart. Listening to your mate shows that you not only care about what is being said, but also that you care about *your partner*. While the importance of listening is clear, many of us have trouble actually doing it.

Hus is an amazing listener; *most* of the time. There are definitely weeks when I've told him 5 (or 25) times, "we are going to X's house on Saturday night" and when Saturday night rolls around, Hus claims to have never been told about it. It happens. But for the most part, he's wonderful. His superior listening ability is especially good for me because I love to talk. I can talk about anything to anyone. Hus, my parents, and many friends have said that I tend to 'think out loud.' So for me, it's just fabulous that he's a good listener. When he listens, I feel valued. How do

I know that he's listening? He looks at me, gives me feedback, asks me questions, remembers things that I've said, and even seems to understand my train of thought (which can be a very difficult thing to do!). All of these things make me feel like I'm important to him.

Listening is more than just hearing a message. The International Listening Association, a professional organization whose members are dedicated to learning more about the impact that listening has on all human activity, defines listening as "the process of receiving, constructing meaning from, and responding to spoken and/or nonverbal messages." Drs. Andrew Wolvin, Ph.D., and Carolyn Coakley, Ph.D., claim that listening involves receiving, attending to, understanding, responding to, and recalling sounds and visual images from interactions with others.[100]

What are some things that you can do to become a better listener? Based on the definitions above, listening involves more than just collecting information and storing it. You must be actively engaged in the conversation. You should not only hear the message, but you also need to respond to it. When talking with your loved ones, consider these strategies to show that you are actively listening:

- *Maintain eye contact with your partner.* Looking at your partner when he or she is talking is not only a great way to show that you are listening, but long gazes with a significant other have been shown to increase feelings of intimacy and trust in relationships.

- *Nod your head and/or smile to show understanding.* This type of positive feedback is very important when listening. Nodding and smiling when your partner is talking encourages your partner to share his or her feelings and thoughts.

- *Ask questions when you don't understand.* Don't let your partner tell his or her entire story if you don't understand what they're talking about. You may think that asking questions is rude; but in most situations, probing further while someone is speaking can show that you care about understanding their message. Saying, "what did you mean when you said X?," can help you better understand what is being said. Additionally, asking questions like, "how did that make you feel?" can help your partner explore his or her feelings, which can also show your mate that you care about what they say.

- *Provide positive vocal feedback* (such as "uh-hu," "that makes sense," "okay," or "yeah"). Providing positive vocal feedback can enhance a speaker's confidence and generate positive emotions.[101] Not including positive vocal feedback can result in speakers hesitating or even stopping to ask why you're not listening. When providing any kind of feedback, make sure that your feedback is obvious, appropriate, clear, and immediate.[102]

So, listen up when your significant other is talking. It could be the difference between him or her feeling loved or feeling ignored.

♥

DISH OUT SOME R-E-S-P-E-C-T

Researchers have surveyed individuals who have been married for over fifty years and have discovered that there are only a few common characteristics that these long-lasting relationships share.[103] One of the most reported features of these couples is that they value having respect for one another.

"Respect goes a long way. If you both respect each other, you will respect your partner's career choice, lifestyle, needs and wants, values... the list goes on and on. Finding value in that person and who they are and what they believe in sets a good foundation for relationships. Respect is what I believe makes a good partnership."

-Amanda, in a relationship with Fernando since July 2002 & married since September 2007

Respectful people value their partners. They treat each other with dignity and *never* demean one another, especially for personal gain or amusement. They don't have parent-child communication interactions with one another. They love their partners for who they are and not for who they want them to be. And, they respect their partners' space, hobbies, and careers. Plain and simple: respect your mate (and it wouldn't be such a bad idea to respect other people, too).

♥

ACCEPT

When Hus and I first met, we clicked rather quickly. We just seemed to mesh well together. And, for about a year after beginning to date, I thought that Hus *and* our relationship were absolutely perfect. We loved everything about one another, we hardly ever fought, and to top it all off, we were one of those mushy couples. You know, the ones you gag at in public? We were one of *those* couples. Everything was great and no one could have told us differently.

Then, about a year into our courtship, we started to notice all of the little things about one another that we didn't like, found to be annoying, and could have even been deal-breakers. When we moved in together, these things (and others) became even more noticeable. Over the years, these irritants have caused many arguments and a good deal of conflict in our relationship. I wanted to change Hus and he wanted to change me. We both wanted one another to mold into these perfect, idealized people. What a mistake. What a HUGE mistake.

It is completely unrealistic to think that anyone is perfect or has the potential to be perfect. If you've met a perfect person, give me a call. Seriously, call me because that person should be on the news or in a history book or something. It's additionally impractical to believe that you somehow have the ability to create the perfect partner. Recognizing your partner's flaws

> "I think it's important to realize that in addition to all the wonderful things about your partner, there are also going to be things that drive you crazy and that's okay—it's what makes them them!"
>
> -Elizabeth, in a relationship with Mark since December 1997 and married since November 2002

(everyone has them) and accepting your mate for who he or she is (good *and* bad) is a major component of healthy relationships. You **cannot** change your mate. If by chance the behavior, personality trait, or habit that irks you is beyond your acceptance, you may need to seriously reevaluate your partnership.

When Hus and I came to the realization that we could not change one another, we grew closer as a couple. I love him for who he is and he loves me for who I am, regardless of the fact that he is consistently late and I am habitually bossy.

♥

TRUST YOUR MATE

It probably comes as no surprise that one of the most important characteristics of true intimacy in any great relationship is trust. We need to trust that our partner will keep our deepest darkest secrets private, always be there for us when we need someone to listen to our problems, help us pick up the pieces when our world comes crashing down, and will not intentionally screw us over or hurt our feelings.

> "One of the most important things in our relationship is trust. We trust each other to make the right (or to the best of our knowledge) decisions about whatever crops up."
>
> *-Debby, married to John since December 1970*

"As partners develop increased trust in one another, they are likely to become increasingly dependent on one another--that is, they are likely to become increasingly satisfied, increasingly willing to forgo alternatives, and increasingly willing to invest in the relationship."[104] When individuals trust their partners, they feel safe, secure, and content.

What affects trust in our relationships? Researcher Dr. Susan Boon, Ph.D., identified four key issues that impact the development of trust, which include dependability, responsiveness, faith, and conflict resolution.[105]

- Dependable partners are always there for each other when one or both of them are in need. Whether partners are happy or sad, healthy or sick, or rich or poor (sound familiar), dependable partners will be there for each other through thick and thin.

- Individuals should also be responsive and sensitive to their partners' needs. Responsive partners are willing to sacrifice their own needs for the needs of their partners. Additionally, responsive partners are willing to help their partners achieve their goals; even if that sometimes means that their own goals have to be put on hold.

- Faithfulness is also important. Faithful partners are in it for the long haul. Not only are faithful partners not going to leave or cheat on each other, but they are also not consumed by the fear that their mates will leave them or that their mates are cheating on them. Furthermore, faithful partners are not jealous of the relationships their mates have with opposite- or same-sex friends.

- Lastly, couples need to be able to resolve conflicts effectively, which involves being collaborative and constructive. "If partners tend to withdraw from potential conflicts, constantly give in to preserve the peace, or force their goals on each other, trust weakens."[106]

These four characteristics combine to enhance feelings of trust in relationships. So, if you want to work on building or maintaining trust with your mate, you need to be there for your partner whenever he or she needs you, have faith in your relationship and in your mate, be responsive to your partner's needs, and be willing to work towards actually resolving conflict. And, always remember that trust is key to a healthy relationship.

"At this point, it sounds cliché, but when you've been in a relationship without trust, it becomes the biggest thing you cherish when you finally have it. With trust, you have freedom in your relationship, you have peace of mind, and you have an intense and continuous respect for your significant other knowing without a shadow of a doubt, you can always trust him or her."

-Heather, in a relationship with Justin since May 2008

Conclusion

"Try everything to save your marriage, even things that you don't think will work. If everything doesn't work or your partner refuses to try anything, consider divorce. No one deserves to be stuck in a miserable marriage—not even you."

-Alisa Bowman, author of
Project Happily Ever After: Saving Your Marriage When the Fairytale Falters

No relationship is perfect. No relationship is void of conflict. No relationship experiences happiness every second of every day.

All relationships have their ups and downs. All relationships take effort from both people involved to succeed. All relationships have potential.

True love is possible. And, all of you deserve true love. Supportive, adoring, open, exciting, euphoric, hilarious, erotic, affectionate, compelling, amazingly demanding and stressful love. Yeah, that kind of love. That's the good stuff.

But in order to get that, you can't give up. If it's worth it, you need to try everything. *Everything.* Using the tips found in this book, on a consistent basis, can help you. But you have to work at it. There's no quick fix. Relationships are continuous, and so the work that you put into them needs to also be continuous.

~~~~~

The rest of this conclusion is for those of you who have reached a not-so-great point in your relationship. If you feel like you're at a crossroad, like things aren't that great anymore, or like they're downright bad, keep reading.

Once a couple realizes that they have reached this point, they have to make some tough decisions. Why has our relationship taken a turn for the worse? Can I deal with the causes of our dissatisfaction? Are these problems fixable? Are we motivated to do the work? Is this relationship worth saving? Should I stay or should I go?

If you've been at this place (or if you're currently living there), these questions have likely crossed your mind 1, 2, or a gazillion times. And, you have likely become overwhelmed by them. These are tough choices to make. Maybe you don't want to think about this stuff or maybe you've just become so used to the way things are that you don't want to do anything. Well, before you decide to throw in the towel, try these three ideas.

STEP ONE: FIGURE IT OUT

Sit down and determine what's really going on. Why is your relationship status in limbo? What has your partner done? What have YOU done? Why do you think the two of you have behaved in this manner? Write these things down. Make this list include very specific things that have been bothering you about your partner and your relationship. Write about things that your mate has done in your relationship and how he or she has made YOU feel. Then take a few minutes to categorize these behaviors by answering the following sentence for each offense:

"In the grand scheme of things,
that was _____."

Were the behaviors in question specific or general, significant or trivial, important or unimportant, hurtful or annoying? Lastly, figure out if you would ever be able to forgive and forget (i.e. get over) these actions if your mate sincerely apologized for them.

STEP TWO: MAKE A LOVE LIST

Make a list of reasons why you love your partner. Think about why you started dating, what he or she has done in the past to make you happy, and maybe most importantly, what he or she *still* does to make you happy. Why were you initially drawn to your mate? Maybe you love your partner because he or she has some admirable personality traits or because your mate does things for you or because your partner is smokin' hot; I mean, has a great smile. Whatever the reason, write it down. Sometimes, thinking about why you liked your relationship in the beginning stages can help rekindle some of those feelings and maybe help you appreciate your partner now.

STEP THREE: CREATE AN "IF" LIST

Now it's time to develop an "I would absolutely love our relationship if" list. Write down things that you would like to see change. Write down some specific "directions." Make a set of directions for your partner AND a set of directions for yourself. For example, "I would really like to hear that you love me more often," "I need to work on complimenting you," "I wish that you would put me first and actually want to hang out with me," "I want to love you unconditionally and for you to do the same for me," "I want to hold you at night and know that no one else is on your mind" are great projections for the future of your relationship. Remember that it's not just your partner who needs to change- you likely need to change as well. Just as it takes two to fix a broken relationship, it probably also took two to break your relationship in the first place.

Once you've created these lists, share them with your partner. Tell your mate that you'd like to talk about some things. Set aside an hour or two to talk. With no distractions. Tell your mate that you created a few lists that you'd like to share. Say that you'd like to read the lists without any interruptions and that you'd like him/her to really listen to what you have to say. Share your lists and then talk about them together. Ask your partner how he or she would complete some of the sentences that you completed. What would be on your mate's "love list"? Also, talk about what each of you can do to fix things. And, if you think that your relationship is not fixable, **calmly** discuss where your relationship will go next.

I can't promise you that this conversation will save your relationship, but it might at least give you an idea about where you want to go with it. The point here is: don't give up, unless you've already tried everything.

BLOGS FOR COUPLES

Jen's Love Lessons
www.JensLoveLessons.com

Helping you keep the spark alive in your relationship with real relationship advice based on an interesting mix of real life experiences and real relationship research is the intention of my own blog. In my blog, I cover a wide variety of topics related to relationship initiation, maintenance, and dissolution including, actively listening, increasing intimacy, managing conflict, being supportive, breaking up, flirting, holding interesting conversations with others, sex, communication skills, and many more. In fact, many of the posts on my blog informed the content in this very book.

Project Happily Ever After
www.ProjectHappilyEverAfter.com

Alisa Bowman is the author of this blog and quite possibly my all-time favorite relationship book of the same name. She is brilliant. You will love her blog. Enough said.

Making Love Sustainable
www.Daily.GoodCleanLove.com

Wendy Strgar, the Chairwoman and Founder of Good Clean Love (a business which offers all natural love products and educational resources), writes this blog. Let me just say that she's amazing. If you like to read eloquent, vivid, creative writing, then reading her blog should be part of your daily routine. Wendy is one of the better writers I know (and I'm surrounded by writers). Her intuitiveness about the dynamics of relationships and sex amazes me.

Married Man Sex Life
www.MarriedManSexLife.com

As he describes himself on his blog, "Athol Kay is an innovative thinker, humorist, and family man with a one track mind." While some of his comments are a teeny bit sexist, his wittiness makes me forget about all that men-and-women-are-from-different-planets-and-therefore-cannot-communicate-with-one-another nonsense. Regardless, he gives some concrete advice and much of it is backed up by psychological and sociological ideas. A good read indeed.

Simple Marriage:
a better marriage by keeping it simple
www.SimpleMarriage.net

The author of Simple Marriage, Dr. Corey Allan, Ph.D., is a Marriage and Family Therapist with a passion for helping couples realize their true potential. As explained on his website, "Marriage is more about becoming a better human than it is about the two people being happy. And when you keep things simple, you can experience more in marriage and life." He tackles real issues that arise in marriage, throws in a little of his own real life experiences, and provides his readers with practical advice, which make his website one of my all-time favorites.

The Married Bed:
Sex and Intimacy for Married Christians
www.TheMarriageBed.com

This informative website "provides a Christian alternative for married and engaged couples seeking information about marital intimacy." The authors, Paul and Lori, clearly, thoroughly, and sensitively discuss the Bible's views on marriage, male and female biology, sexual problems, suggestions for marital sexual exploration, and a huge discussion forum where you can add in your own two cents on a wide variety of topics.

Therapy Notes
www.GroupTherapyAssociates.org/blog

Creators Esther and Llouana are "just a couple regular gals with a passion for helping others," as explained on their site. These women combine their personal and professional experiences (Llouana is a Licensed Professional Counselor and a National Certified Counselor, while Esther is a Licensed Marriage and Family Therapist) to write about the trails, tribulations, and joys that come with love, marriage, and parenting.

The Dating Divas:
Strengthening Marriages, One Date at a Time
www.TheDatingDivas.com

These 11 happily married women write about how to keep your relationship alive and kicking by going on unique dates. And they have a TON of ideas for you! They have dates for just the two of you, four or more people, and all of the theme dates you can think of (and a lot you've never thought of). They're creative and entertaining.

Marriage Gems:
Research-Based Marriage Tips & Insights
www.LifeGems4Marriage.com

Like myself, Lori Lowe, the creator of Marriage Gems, also uses academic research to back up her writing. I enjoy reading Lori's posts and especially a few of her series including her *Research-Based Love Tips* series on Mondays, her *Happy Life, Happy Marriage* series on Wednesdays, her *Keeping the Spark Alive* series on Fridays.

BOOKS FOR COUPLES

Project: Happily Ever After
Saving Your Marriage When the Fairy Tale Falters
Author: Alisa Bowman

Project Happily Ever After: Saving Your Marriage When the Fairytale Falters by the amazingly eloquent Alisa Bowman is one of the best books I have read in a very, *very* long time. This book is definitely on my 10-relationship-books-you-should-read-before-you-die list. Yep, I went there. Now are you ready to take me seriously?

Many of you might be thinking: "I have a great relationship, why would *I* need to read this book?" That's actually the mindset I was in when it arrived on my doorstep. And then I quickly realized that **this is not just a save-your-failing-marriage book**. No sir. I mean, don't get me wrong- this is a wonderfully insightful book for individuals who need a little or a ton of help with their marriages, but it's also a love story; an incredibly inspirational love story. And, the best part is that this love story is being told to you by your new BFF, Alisa Bowman. I say that because that's how she makes you feel as a reader. Somehow, she understands what you're going through in your own relationship- the good, the bad, and the ugly- and she tells you intimate details about her own relationship. Alisa let's you into her world and it's shocking how similar the two of you are. Her perception of marriage is spot-on to what I (and many of you) have felt or will feel as you navigate through love, marriage, and child- raising.

The book reads like a really interesting story from your favorite fairytale with chapters that tell Alisa's voyage from being a single fair maiden, meeting her prince, having her prince turn into an inconsiderate frog, starting a project, and having her frog turn back into a prince. As the book description states, "It bravely tells the story of how [Alisa] went from wishing her husband dead to renewing her wedding vows." It truly is a happily ever after story.

There were several aspects of this book that either deeply moved me, made me take a step back and think for a minute (or ten), caused me to laugh out loud, or intrigued me to continue reading. *Project Happily Ever After* is definitely a book I LOVE. You will also love this book. Yes, each and every one of you. I'm certain of it. So, get in a comfy chair, relax, and enjoy the journey- Alisa's journey.

Love That Works: A Guide to Enduring Intimacy
Author: Wendy Strgar

In 2008, I went to an academic conference for the Society for the Scientific Study of Sexuality (SSSS). I was presenting a paper about taking a message production approach to studying condom negotiation... yadda yadda yadda... and I met a woman who was promoting her small business. She was charming, smart, and passionate about love, sex, and relationships. She was interesting. We had a few conversations here and there and before I left, I bought some of her products. This woman was Wendy Strgar, the founder of *Good Clean Love* (a business which offers all natural love products and educational resources). Over the years, I've loved reading her blog and buying more *Good Clean Love* products.

Wendy recently wrote her first book and when she asked me to review it, I enthusiastically agreed. *Love That Works: A Guide to Enduring Intimacy* is an insightful, eloquent book about the organic components of sustainable love. Her book is about acceptance, partnership, fulfillment, oh yeah, and sex. Wendy discusses the complexities of relationships, and it is through her discussion of these ups and downs that you realize what true love is. Wendy artfully combines her vast knowledge about love and relationships with stories about other couples and her own experiences with her 25-year marriage.

As I was reading her book, there were many instances where I was intrigued, inspired, and touched by her words. I would find myself writing down snippets in my bedside notebook or highlighting and underlining quotes in her book. For instance, in one chapter, Wendy talks about how it can be hard to love people because "collectively, we are all pretty annoying." She's right. We are all pretty darn annoying! She ends this section with a suggestion: "Let's just go forward admitting how annoying and flawed we all are, so that we aren't surprised when living together becomes challenging. We will all go in knowing that we are choosing to get over it, and in doing so, we'll find these brief yet life-changing moments of holding on to what we all want the most: each other" (p. 37). How can you not LOVE that? As my friend Marti would say, her words are glorious. Her insight about the inner-workings of relationships astounds me. In the end, Wendy's writing is multilayered, absorbing, motivational, and profound. You will **love** this book.

Fight Less, Love More:
5-Minute Conversations to Change Your
Relationship without Blowing Up or Giving In
Author: Laurie Puhn, J. D.

Four words: I LOVE THIS BOOK! I actually can't get over how much I love it. It's right up my alley. I even bought a few extra copies for a few of my married BFFs. It's absolutely great.

Let's just start with the first 5-minute conversation. "Tame Rudeness: Install a Daily Communication Routine" is a chapter that several million people would benefit from reading. Here, Laurie talks about "new rude" relationships, which are characterized by indifference and neglect. To help these couples, Laurie suggests that five sentences be incorporated into the couple's daily communication routine including to, say hello and good-bye to your mate, start the day by saying "good morning," end the day by saying "good night," tell your mate at least once a day one reason for your love ("I love you because…"), and give a compliment. These simple, yet extremely powerful, exchanges can seriously impact your relationship satisfaction.

Practical, feasible, and thorough, *Fight Less, Love More* is one of the better relationship books I've read in a long while. Laurie sensitively addresses many relational communication issues from inspiring appreciation to keeping some things in your relationship private to breaking free from stubbornness to combating negativity that many couples have become accustomed to. And even better: this is a great book for anyone in any relationship stage including couples who have yet to experience any dissatisfaction all the way to couples who feel like they might just have to throw in the towel. This book will help you; all of you. Seriously.

OTHER BOOKS
YOU HAVE TO READ

Pure Romance Between the Sheets by Patty Brisben

Things I Wish I'd Known Before We Got Married by Dr. Gary Chapman, Ph.D.

Hot Monogamy: Essential Steps to More Passionate, Intimate Lovemaking by Dr. Patricia Love, M.D.

The 5 Love Languages: The Secret to Love That Lasts by Dr. Gary Chapman, Ph.D.

"To love somebody is not
just a strong feeling.
It is a decision.
It is a judgment.
It is a promise."

-Erich Fromm

references

[1] Beach, S. R. H., & Gupta, M. (2006). Directive and nondirective spousal support: Differential Effects? *Journal of Marital and Family Therapy, 32*, 465-477. Mickelson, K. D., Claffey, S. T., & Williams, S. L. (2006). The moderating role of gender and gender role attitudes on the link between spousal support and well-being. *Sex Roles, 55*, 73-82.

[2] Logsdon, M. C., & Usui, W. (2001). Psychosocial predictors of postpartum depression in diverse groups of women. *Western Journal of Nursing Research, 23*, 563-574.

[3] Burleson, B. R. (1994). Comforting messages: Features, functions, and outcomes. In J. A. Daly & J. M. Wiemann (Eds.), *Strategic interpersonal communication* (pp. 135-161). Hillsdale, NJ: Lawrence Erlbaum Associates.

[4] Burleson, B. R. (2003). Emotional support skill. In J. O. Greene & B. R. Burleson (Eds.), *Handbook of communication and social interaction skills* (pp. 551-594). Mahwah, N: Lawrence Erlbaum Associates.

[5] Burleson, B. R. (1990). Comforting as everyday social support: Relational consequences of supportive behaviors. In S. Duck and R. C. Silver's (Eds.), *Personal relationships and social support* (pp. 66-82). London: Sage.

[6] Acitelli, L. K. (1996). The neglected links between marital support and marital satisfaction. In G. R. Pierce, B. R. Sarason, & I. G. Sarason (Eds.), *Handbook of social support and the family* (pp. 83-104). New York: Plenum Press. Samter, W. (1994). Unsupportive relationships: Deficiencies in the support giving skills of the lonely person's friends. In B. R. Burleson, T. L. Albrecht, & I. G. Sarason (Eds.), *The communication of social support: Messages, interactions, relationships, and community* (pp. 195-214). Thousand Oaks, CA: Sage.

[7] Cutrona, C. E., & Russell, D. (1987). The provisions of social relationships and adaptations to stress. In W. H. Jones & D. Perlman (Eds.), *Advances in personal relationships* (Vol. 1, pp. 37-67). Greenwich, CT: JAI Press. Xu, Y., & Burleson, B. R. (2001). Effects of sex, culture, and support type on perceptions of spousal social support: An assessment of the "support gap" hypothesis in early marriage. *Human Communication Research, 27,* 535-566.

[8] Prager, J. K. (1995). *The psychology of intimacy.* New York: Guilford Press.

[9] Doohan, E.-A., M., & Manusov, V. (2004). The communication of compliments in romantic relationships: An investigation of relational satisfaction and sex differences and similarities in compliment behavior. *Western Journal of Communication, 68,* 170-194. Prager, J. K. (1995). *The psychology of intimacy.* New York: Guilford Press.

[10] Doohan, E.-A., M., & Manusov, V. (2004). The communication of compliments in romantic relationships: An investigation of relational satisfaction and sex differences and similarities in compliment behavior. *Western Journal of Communication, 68,* 170-194.

[11] Murray, S. L., Holmes, J. G., & Griffin, D. W. (2000). Self-esteem and the quest for felt security: How perceived regard regulates attachment processes. *Journal of Personality and Social Psychology, 78,* 478–498.

[12] Marigold, D. C., Holmes, J. G., & Ross, M. (2007). More than words: Reframing compliments from romantic partners fosters security in low self-esteem individuals. *Journal of Personality and Social Psychology, 92,* 232-248.

[13] Marigold, D. C., Holmes, J. G., & Ross, M. (2007). More than words: Reframing compliments from romantic partners fosters security in low self-esteem individuals. *Journal of Personality and Social Psychology, 92,* 232-248. Quote from p. 232.

[14] Baxter, L. A., & Philpott, J. (1982). Attribution-based strategies for initiating and terminating relationships. *Communication Quarterly, 30,* 217-224. Cialdini, R. B. (1993). Influence: Science and practice (3rd ed.). New York: HarperCollins.

[15] Berger, C. R., Gardner, R. R., Parks, M. R., Shulman, L., & Miller, G. R. (1976). Interpersonal epistemology and interpersonal communication. In G. R. Miller (Ed.), *Explorations in interpersonal communication* (pp. 149-172). Beverly Hills, CA: Sage.

[16] Remmer, A., Shirzadi, A., Greenberg, J., Vaughn, C. (2011). Technologically-mediated romance: An analysis of complimenting behaviors via Facebook. *Unpublished manuscript created for class project at James Madison University.*

[17] Wolfson, N., & Manes, J. (1980). The compliment as a social strategy. *Papers in Linguistics: International Journal of Human Communication, 13*, 391-410.

[18] Burleson, B. R. (1995). Personal relationships as a skilled accomplishment. *Journal of Social and Personal Relationships, 12*, 575-581. Chesney, A. P., Blakeney, P. E., Cole, C. M., & Chan, F. A. (1981). A comparison of couples who have sought sex therapy with couples who have not. Journal of Sex and Marital Therapy, 7, 131-140. Ferroni, R, & Taffee, J. (1997). Women's emotional well-being: The importance of communicating sexual needs. *Sexual and Marital Therapy, 12*, 127-138.

[19] Dindia, K., & Timmerman, L. (2003). Accomplishing romantic relationships. In J. O. Greene & B. R. Burleson (Eds.), *Handbook of communication and social interaction skills.* Mahwah, NJ: Lawrence Erlbaum.

[20] Hicks, A. M., & Diamond, L. M. (2008). How was your day? Couples' affect when telling and hearing daily events. *Personal Relationships, 15*, 205-228.

[21] Hicks, A. M., & Diamond, L. M. (2008). How was your day? Couples' affect when telling and hearing daily events. *Personal Relationships, 15*, 205-228.

[22] Verderber, K. S., Verderber, R. F., & Berryman-Fink, C. (2007). *Inter-act: Interpersonal communication concepts, skills, and contexts* (11th edition). New York: Oxford University Press.

[23] Aron, A., Melinat, E., Aron, E. N., Vallone, R. D., & Bator, R. J. (1997). The experimental generation of interpersonal closeness: A procedure and some preliminary findings. *Personality and Social Psychology Bulletin, 23*, 363-377.

[24] Baxter, L.A., & Wilmot, W. (1984). "Secret tests": Strategies for acquiring information about the state of the relationship. *Human Communication Research, 11*, 171-201.

[25] Andersen, J. (2001). Financial problems as predictors of divorce: A social exchange perspective. *Proceedings for the Western Region Home Management/ Family Economics Educators.*

[26] Baxter, L. A., & Philpott, J. (1982). Attribution-based strategies for initiating and terminating relationships. *Communication Quarterly, 30*, 217-224. Bell, R. A., & Daly, J. A. (1984). The affinity-seeking function in communication. *Communication Monographs, 51*, 91-115.

[27] Clark, C. L., Shaver, P. R., & Abrahams, A. (1999). Strategic behaviors in romantic relationships. *Personality and Social Psychology Bulletin, 25*, 709-722.

[28] Dindia, K., & Baxter, L. A. (1987). Strategies for maintaining and repairing marital relationships. *Journal of Social and Personal Relationships, 4*, 143-158.

[29] Dunn, E. W., Huntsinger, J., Lun, J., & Sinclair, S. (2008). The gift of similarity: How good and bad gifts influence relationships. *Social Cognition, 26*, 469-481.

[30] Aspinwall, L. G., & Taylor, S. E. (1992). Modeling cognitive adaptation: A longitudinal investigation of the impact of individual differences and coping on college adjustment and performance. *Journal of Personality and Social Psychology, 63*, 989-1003. Taylor, S. E., Kemeny, M. E., Reed, G. M., Bower, J. E., & Gruenewald, T. L. (2000). Psychological resources, positive illusions, and health. *American Psychologist, 55*, 99-109.

[31] Dicke, A. K. (1998). *Optimism and its effect on romantic relationships.* (Doctoral dissertation). Texas Tech University, Texas.

[32] Berger, C. R., & Bell, R. A. (1988). Plans and the initiation of social relationships. *Human Communication Research, 15*, 217-235.

[33] Helgeson, V. S. (1994). The effects of self-beliefs and relationship beliefs on adjustment to a relationship stressor. *Personal Relationships, 1*, 241–258. Murray, S. L., & Holmes, J. G. (1997). A leap of faith? Positive illusions in romantic relationships. *Personality and Social Psychology Bulletin, 23*, 586-604.

[34] Srivastava, S., McGoingal, K. M., Richards, J. M., Butler, E. A., & Gross, J. J. (2006). Optimism in close relationships: How seeing things in a positive light makes them so. *Journal of Personality and Social Psychology, 91*, 143-153.

[35] Carver, C. S., Kus, L. A., & Scheier, M. F. (1994). Effects of good versus bad mood and optimistic versus pessimistic outlook on social acceptance versus rejection. Journal of Social and Clinical Psychology, 13, 138-151. Hewleg-Larson, M., Sadeghian, P., & Webb, M. S. (2002). The stigma of being pessimistically biased. *Journal of Social and Clinical Psychology, 21*, 92-107.

[36] Hewleg-Larson, M., Sadeghian, P., & Webb, M. S. (2002). The stigma of being pessimistically biased. *Journal of Social and Clinical Psychology, 21*, 92-107.

[37] Furr, R. M., & Funder, D. C. (1998). A multi-modal analysis of personal negativity. *Journal of Personality and Social Psychology, 74*, 1580-1591.

[38] Crocker, J., Major, B., & Steele, C. (1998). Social stigma. In D. Gilbert, S. T. Fiske, and G. Lindsay (Eds.), *The handbook of social psychology* (4th edition, Vol. 2, pp. 504-553). New York: McGraw Hill.

[39] Baumeister, R.F., Bratslavsky, E., Finkenauer, C., & Vohs, K.D. (2001). Bad is stronger than good. *Review of General Psychology, 5*, 323-370.

[40] Ellis-Christensen, T. (2010). *What is the negativity bias?* Retrieved from www.WiseGeek.com.

[41] Murray, S. L., Holmes, J. G., & Griffin, D. W. (2000). Self-esteem and the quest for felt security: How perceived regard regulates attachment processes. *Journal of Personality and Social Psychology, 78*, 478-498. Rusbult, C. E., Verette, J., Whitney, G. A., Slovik, L. F., & Lipkus, I. (1991). Accommodation processes in close relationships: Theory and preliminary empirical evidence. *Journal of Personality and Social Psychology, 43*, 230, 242.

[42] Neff, L. A., & Karney, B. R. (2005). Gender differences in social support: A question of skills or responsiveness? *Journal of Personality and Social Psychology, 88*, 79-90.

[43] Bradbury, T. N., & Fincham, F. D. (1990). Attributions in marriage: Review and critique. *Psychological Bulletin, 107*, 3-33.

[44] McNulty, J. K., O'Mara, E. M., & Karney, B. R. (2008). Benevolent cognitions as a strategy of relationship maintenance: "Don't sweat the small stuff"...But it is not all small stuff. *Journal of Personality and Social Psychology, 94*, 631-646.

[45] Bazzini, D. G., Stack, E. R., Martincin, P. D., & Davis, C. P. (2007). The effects of reminiscing about laughter on relationship satisfaction. *Motivation and Emotion, 31*, 25- 34. Ziv, A. (1988). Humor's role in married life. *Humor, 1*, 223- 229. Ziv, A., & Gadish, O. (1989). Humor in marital satisfaction. *The Journal of Social Psychology, 129*, 759- 768.

[46] Gottman, J., Coan, J., Swanson, C., & Carrere, S. (1998). Predicting marital happiness and stability from newlywed interactions. *Journal of Marriage and the Family, 60*, 5–22.

[47] Carstensen, L., Gottman, J., & Levenson, R. (1995). Emotional behavior in long-term marriage. *Psychology and Aging, 10*, 140–149.

[48] Lauer, R. Lauer, J., & Kerr, S. T. (1990). The long-term marriage: Perceptions of stability and satisfaction. *International Journal of Aging and Human Development, 30*, 189- 195.

[49] Bazzini, D. G., Stack, E. P., Martinicin, P. D., & Davis, C. (2007). "Remember when we...?": The effects of reminiscing about laughter on relationship satisfaction. *Motivation and Emotion, 31*, 25-34.

[50] Campbell, L., Martin, R. A., & Ward, J. R. (2008). An observational

study of humor while resolving conflict in dating couples. *Personal Relationships, 15*, 41-55.

[51] Campbell, L., Martin, R. R., & Ward, J. R. (2008). An observational study of humor use while resolving conflict in dating couples. *Personal Relationships, 15*, 41-55.

[52] Martin, R. A., Puhlik-Doris, P., Larsen, G., Gray, L., & Weir, K. (2003). Individual differences in uses of humor and their relation to psychological well-being: Development of the Humor Styles Questionnaire. *Journal of Research in Personality, 37*, 48-75.

[53] Campbell, L., Martin, R. R., & Ward, J. R. (2008). An observational study of humor use while resolving conflict in dating couples. *Personal Relationships, 15*, 41-55. Quote from p. 42

[54] Feldman, H. A., Johannes, C. B., McKinlay, J. B., & Longcope, C. (1998). Low dehydroepiandrosterone sulfate and heart disease in middle-aged men: Cross-sectional results from the Massachusetts male aging study. *Annals of Epidemiology, 8*, 217- 228. Smith, D. A., Ness, E. M., Herbert, R., Schechter, C. B., Phillips, R. A., Diamond, J. A. & Landrigan, P. J. (2005). Abdominal diameter index: A more powerful anthropometric measure of prevalent coronary heart disease risk in adult males. *Diabetes Obesity Metabolism, 7*, 370-380.

[55] Palmore, E. (1982). Predictors of the longevity difference: A twenty-five year follow-up. *The Gerontologist, 22*, 513- 518. Persson, G. (1981). Five-year mortality in a 70-year-old urban population in relation to psychiatric diagnosis, personality, sexuality and early prenatal death. *Acta Psychiatrica Scandinavica, 64*, 244-253. Smith, D. S., Frankel, S., & Yarnell, J. (1997). Sex and death: Are they related? *British Medical Journal, 314*, 1641-1645. Starr, B. D., & Weiner, M. B. (1981). *The Starr-Weiner report on sex and sexuality in the mature years.* New York: Stein and Day Publishers.

[56] Bagley, C., & Tremblay, B. (1997). Suicidal behaviors in homosexual and bisexual males. *Crisis, 18*, 24-34. Catania, J. A., & White, C. B. (1982). Sexuality in an aged sample: Cognitive determinants of masterbation. *Archives of Sexual Behavior, 11*, 237-245. Gallup, G., Burch, R. L., & Platek, S. M. (2002). Does semen have antidepressant properties? *Archives of Sexual Behavior, 31*, 289- 293.

[57] Hurlbert, D. F., & Whittaker, K. E. (1991). The role of masturbation in marital and sexual satisfaction: A comparative study of female masturbators and nonmasturbators. *Journal of Sex Education & Therapy, 17*, 272- 282.

[58] Odent, M. (1999). *The scientification of love.* London, UK: Free Association Books Limited. Weeks, D. J. (2002). Sex for the amateur adult: Health,

self-esteem and countering ageist stereotypes. *Sexual and Relationship Therapy, 17*, 231- 240.

[59] Dunn, K. M., Jordan, K., Croft, P. R., & Assendelft, W. J. J. (2002). Systematic review of sexual problems: Epidemiology and methodology. *Journal of Sex and Marital Therapy, 28*, 399- 422.

[60] Butzer, B., & Campbell, L. (2008). Adult attachment, sexual satisfaction, and relationship satisfaction: A study of married couples. *Personal Relationships, 15*, 141-154. Byers, E. S. (2005). Relationship satisfaction and sexual satisfaction: A longitudinal study of individuals in long-term relationships. *Journal of Sex Research, 42*, 113- 118. Nelson, C. J., Choi, J. M., Mulhall, J. P., & Roth, A. J. (2007). Determinants of sexual satisfaction in men with prostate cancer. *Journal of Sexual Medicine, 5*, 1422-1427. Peck, S. R., Shaffer, D. R., & Williamson, G. M. (2004). Sexual satisfaction and relationship satisfaction in dating couples: The contributions of relationship community and favorability of sexual exchanges. *Journal of Psychology and Human Sexuality, 16*, 17-37.

[61] Tracy, J. K., & Junginger, J. (2007). Correlates of lesbian sexual functioning. *Journal of Women's Health, 16*, 499-509.

[62] Edwards, J. N., & Booth, A. (1994). Sexuality, marriage, and well-being: The middle years. In A. S. Rossi (Ed.), *Sexuality across the life course* (pp. 233-259). Chicago: The University of Chicago Press. Oggins, J., Leber, D., & Veroff, J. (1993). Race and gender differences in black and white newlyweds' perceptions of sexual and marital relationships. *The Journal of Sex Research, 30*, 152-160. Sprecher, S. (2002). Sexual satisfaction in premarital relationships: Associations with satisfaction, love, commitment, and stability. *The Journal of Sex Research, 3*, 1-7. White, L., & Keith, B. (1990). The effect of shift work on the quality and stability of marital relationships. *Journal of Marriage and the Family, 52*, 453- 462.

[63] Oggins, J., Leber, D., & Veroff, J. (1993). Race and gender differences in black and white newlyweds' perceptions of sexual and marital relationships. *The Journal of Sex Research, 30*, 152-160.

[64] Edwards, J. N., & Booth, A. (1994). Sexuality, marriage, and well-being: The middle years. In A. S. Rossi (Ed.), *Sexuality across the life course* (pp. 233-259). Chicago: The University of Chicago Press.

[65] Cleek, M. G., & Pearson, T. A. (1985). Perceived causes of divorce: An analysis of interrelationships. *Journal of Marriage and the Family, 47*, 179-183. Hill, C. T., Rubin, Z., & Peplau, L. A. (1976). Breakups before marriage: The end of 103 affairs. *Journal of Social Issues, 32*, 147- 168. Sprecher, S. (1994). Twosides to the breakup of dating relationships. *Personal Relationships, 1*, 199-222.

[66] Byers, E. S. (2005). Relationship satisfaction and sexual satisfaction: A longitudinal study of individuals in long-term relationships. *Journal of Sex*

Research, 42, 113- 118. Byers, E. S., & Demmons, S. (1999). Sexual satisfaction and self disclosure within dating relationships. *The Journal of Sex Research, 36*, 180-189. Chesney, A. P., Blakeney, P. E., Cole, C. M., & Chan, F. A. (1981). A comparison of couples who have sought sex therapy with couples who have not. *Journal of Sex and Marital Therapy, 7*, 131-140. Cupach, W. R., & Metts, S. (1991). Sexuality and communication in close relationships. In K. McKinney & S. Sprecher (Eds.), *Sexuality in close relationships*. Hillsdale, NJ: Lawrence Erlbaum. DeLamater, J., & Friedrich, W.N. (2002). Human sexual development. *The Journal of Sex Research, 39*, 10- 15. Haavio-Mannila, E., & Kontula, O. (1997). Correlates of increased sexual satisfaction. *Archives of Sexual Behavior, 26(4)*, 399-419. MacNeil, S., & Byers, E.S. (1997). The relationship between sexual problems, communication, and sexual satisfaction. *The Canadian Journal of Human Sexuality, 6(4)*, 277-289. Purnine, D.M., & Carey, M. (1999). Dyadic coorientation: Reexamination of a method for studying interpersonal communication. *Archives of Sexual Behavior, 28(1)*, 45-61. Resnick, S. (2002). Sexual pleasure; the next frontier in the study of sexuality. *SIECUS Report, 30*, 6-11. Sprecher, S. & Regan, P.C. (2000). Sexuality in a Relational Context. In C. Hendrick & S. Hendrick (Eds.), *Close Relationships: A Sourcebook* (pp. 245-262). Thousand Oaks: Sage Publications Inc.

[67] Marble, M. (1997, March 31). Americans find it easier to have sex than to talk about it. *Women's Health Weekly*, 13-14.

[68] Gill Rosier, J. (2011). Finding the Love Guru in you: Examining the effectiveness of a sexual coaching skill training program. (Doctoral dissertation). Purdue University, West Lafayette, Indiana.

[69] Floyd, K., Boren, J. P., Hannawa, A. F., Hesse, C., McEwan, B., and Vekslar, A. E. (2009). Kissing in marital and cohabiting relationships: Effects on blood lipids, stress and relationship satisfaction. *Western Journal of Communication, 73*(2), 113-133.

[70] Floyd, K. (2002). Human affection exchange: Attributes of the highly affectionate. *Communication Quarterly, 50*, 135-152. Quote from p. 118.

[71] Anonymous quote.

[72] Canary, D. J., & Stafford, L. (1992). Relational maintenance strategies and equity in marriage. *Communication Monographs, 59*, 243-267.

[73] Stafford, L. (2003). Maintaining romantic relationships: A summary and analysis of one research program. In D. J Canary & M. Dainton (Eds.), *Maintaining relationships through communication: Relational, contextual, and cultural variations* (pp. 51-77). Mahwah, NJ: Erlbaum.

[74] Canary, D. J., & Stafford, L. (1994). Maintaining relationships through strategic and routine interaction. In D. J. Canary & L. Stafford (Eds.), *Communication and relational maintenance* (pp. 3-22). San Diego: Academic Press.

[75] Stafford, L. (2003). Maintaining romantic relationships: A summary and analysis of one research program. In D. J Canary & M. Dainton (Eds.), *Maintaining relationships through communication: Relational, contextual, and cultural variations* (pp. 51-77). Mahwah, NJ: Erlbaum.

[76] Floyd, K., Mikkelson, A. C., Hesse, C., & Pauley, P. M. (2007) Affectionate writing reduces total cholesterol: Two randomized, controlled trials. *Human Communication Research, 33*, 119-142.

[77] Baxter, L.A. (1990). Dialectical contradictions in relationship development. *Journal of Social and Personal Relationships, 7*, 69-88. Rawlins, W. K. (1992). *Friendship matters: Communication, dialectics, and the lifecourse.* Hawthorne, NY: Aldine.

[78] Baxter, L. A. (1987). Symbols of relationship identity in relationship cultures. *Journal of Social and Personal Relationships, 4*, 261-280. Bruess, C. J. S., & Pearson J. C. (1997). Interpersonal rituals in marriage and adult friendship. *Communication Monographs, 64*, 25-46. Bruess, C. J. S., & Pearson, J. C. (2002). The function of mundane ritualizing in adult friendship and marriage. *Communication Research Reports, 19*, 314-326.

[79] Meredith, W., Abbott, D., Lamanna, M., & Sanders, G. (1989). Rituals and family strengths. *Family Perspectives, 23*, 75-83.

[80] Wolin, S. J., & Bennett, L. A. (1984). Family rituals. *Family Process, 23*, 401-420.

[81] Fiese, B. (1992). Dimension of family rituals across two generations: Relation to adolescent identity. *Family Process, 31*, 151-162.

[82] Aron, A., Norman, C., Aron, E., McKenna, C., & Heyman, R. (2000). Couples' shared participation in novel and arousing activities and experienced relationship quality. *Journal of Personality and Social Psychology, 78*, 273-284.

[83] Rothwell, J. (2010). *In the company of others: An introduction to communication.* New York: Oxford University Press.

[84] Schoppe-Sullivan, S. J., Brown, G. L., Cannon, E. A., Mangelsdorf, S. C., & Sokolowski, M. S. (2008). Maternal gatekeeping, coparenting quality, and fathering behavior in families with infants. *Journal of Family Psychology, 22*, 389-398.

[85] Kumashiro, M., Rusbult, C. E., & Finkel, E. J. (2008). Navigating personal and relational concerns: The quest for equilibrium. *Journal of Personality and Social Psychology, 95*, 94- 110.

[86] Kumashiro et al., 2008, p. 94

[87] Kumashiro et al., 2008, p. 95

[88] Baxter, L. A. (1988). A dialectical perspective on communication strategies in relationship development. In S. Duck (Ed.), *Handbook of personal relationships: Theory, research, and interventions* (pp. 257- 273). Chichester, England: Wiley. Baxter, L. A. (1990). Dialectical contradictions in relationship development. *Journal of Social and Personal Relationships, 7*, 69-88. Rawlins, W. K. (1992). *Friendship matters: Communication, dialectics, and the life course.* New York: Aldine de Gruyter.

[89] Baxter, L. A. (1988). A dialectical perspective on communication strategies in relationship development. In S. Duck (Ed.), *Handbook of personal relationships: Theory, research, and interventions* (pp. 257- 273). Chichester, England: Wiley. Baxter, L. A. (1990). Dialectical contradictions in relationship development. *Journal of Social and Personal Relationships, 7*, 69-88. Rawlins, W. K. (1992). *Friendship matters: Communication, dialectics, and the life course.* New York: Aldine de Gruyter.

[90] Petronio, S. (2002). *Boundaries of privacy: Dialectics of disclosure.* New York: State University of New York Press.

[91] Baxter, L. A. (1988). A dialectical perspective on communication strategies in relationship development. In S. Duck (Ed.), *Handbook of personal relationships: Theory, research, and interventions* (pp. 257- 273). Chichester, England: Wiley. Baxter, L. A. (1990). Dialectical contradictions in relationship development. *Journal of Social and Personal Relationships, 7*, 69-88. Rawlins, W. K. (1992). *Friendship matters: Communication, dialectics, and the life course.* New York: Aldine de Gruyter.

[92] Buckingham, D., & Bragg, S. (2003). Young people, media, and personal relationships. Chernin, A. R., & Fishbein, M. (2007, May). *The association between adolescents' exposure to romantic-themed media and the endorsement of unrealistic beliefs about romantic relationships.* Paper presented at the annual meeting of the International Communication Association. San Francisco, CA. Westman, A. S., Lynch, T. J., Lewandowski, L., & Hunt-Carter, E. (2003). Students' use of mass media for ideas about romantic relationships was influenced by by perceived realism of presentation and parental happiness. *Psychological Reports, 92*, 1116- 1118.

[93] Wilmot, W. W., & Hocker, J. L. (2007). *Interpersonal conflict.* New York: McGraw Hill. Lulofs, R. (1994). *Conflict: From theory to action.* Scottsdale, AZ: Gorsuch Scarisbrick.

[94] Fitness, J. (2001). Betrayal, rejection, revenge, and forgiveness: An interpersonal script approach. In M.R. Leary (Ed.). *Interpersonal rejection,* (pp. 73-103). New York: Oxford University Press.

95 Cutrona, C. E. (1996). Social support as a determinant of marital quality: The interplay of negative and supportive behaviors. In G. R. Pierce, B. R. Sarason, & I. G. Sarason (Eds.). *Handbook of social support and the family.* New York: Plenam Press.

96 Birchler, G. R., Weiss, R. L., & Vincent, J. P. (1975). Multimethod analysis of social reinforcement exchange between maritally distressed and nondistressed spouse and stranger dyads. *Journal of Personality and Social Psychology, 31,* 349-360. Gottman, J. M. (1979). *Marital interaction: Experimental investigations.* New York: Academic Press. Margolin, G., & Wompold, B. E. (1981). A sequential analysis of conflict and accord in distressed and nondistressed marital partners. *Journal of Consulting and Clinical Psychology, 49,* 554- 557.

97 Gottman, J. M. (1979). *Marital interaction: Experimental investigations.* New York: Academic Press.

98 Gottman, J., & Silver, N. (1994). Why marriages succeed of fail: How you can make your last. New York: Simon & Schuster.

99 Gottman & Silver (1994), p. 80.

100 Wolvin, A., & Coakley, C. G. (1996). *Listening* (5th edition). Dubuque, IA: Brown & Benchmark.

101 Wolvin & Coakley (1996)

102 Barker, L. L. (1971). *Listening behavior.* Englewood Cliffs, NJ: Prentice-Hall. Daly, J. (1975). *Listening and interpersonal evaluations.* Paper presented at the annual meeting of the Central States Speech Association, Kansas City, MO.

103 Dickson, F. C. (1995). The best is yet to be: Research on long-lasting marriages. In J. T. Wood & S. Duck (Eds.). *Under-studied relationships: Off the beaten track.* (pp. 22-50). Thousand Oaks, CA: Sage.

104 Rusbult, C. E., Olson, N., Davis, J. L., & Hannen, P. A. (2001). Commitment and relationship maintenance mechanisms. In J. Harvey & A. Wenzel (Eds.), *Close romantic relationships: Maintenance and enhancement.* (pp. 87-113). Mahwah, NJ: Erlbaum. Quote from page 107.

105 Boon, S. D. (1994). Dispelling doubt and uncertainty: Trust in romantic relationships. In S. Duck (Eds.), *Dynamics of relationships* (pp. 86-111). Thousand Oaks, CA: Sage.

106 Boon, 1994, p. 98.

About
the Author

Dr. Jennifer Gill Rosier, Ph.D., author of www.JensLoveLessons.com, is an Assistant Professor of Communication Studies at James Madison University. Her broad scholarly research interests include communication skill development and relationship maintenance behaviors. Much of her current research focuses around examining the actual skills needed to effectively communicate about sex in romantic relationships and investigating the role that a wide variety of communication skills play in successful marriages that have experienced hardship (i.e. loss of a child, terminal illness diagnosis, raising multiples, etc.). In the future, she plans to publish two more books based on these two areas of research.

Jennie is married to her favorite person on the planet, has beautiful boy/girl twins, actually likes change and trying new things, tries not to take herself (or life) too seriously, strongly believes that good social scientific research should improve the lives of others and should be accessible to the masses (like through her blog and this book), gets a huge adrenaline rush every time she steps into a classroom at James Madison University, highly enjoys sarcasm, and loves helping others enhance their communication and relationship skills.

Made in the USA
Middletown, DE
28 August 2019